Text by Lindsay Bennett
Principal photographers: Glyn Genin and Pete Bennett
Series Editor: Tony Halliday

Berlitz® POCKET GUIDE

Cancún & Cozumel

Eighth Edition 2003
(Reprinted 2004, 2005, 2006)

PHOTOGRAPHY CREDITS

Pete Bennett 6, 26, 41, 49, 55, 59, 61, 68, 73, 77, 78, 80, 83, 89, 90, 96, 99, 100, 103; Luis Gomez Cardenas 9, 36; Coco Bongo 27; Glyn Genin 11, 19, 21, 22, 29, 30, 32, 34, 37, 39, 44, 46, 47, 52, 58, 62, 63, 64, 87, 91, 92; Tony Halliday 10, 12, 14, 20, 43, 50, 56, 60, 70, 71, 75, 76, 81; Hidden Worlds 86; Marcus Wislon-Smith/Apa 24, 66
Cover picture: Neil Wilson

CONTACTING THE EDITORS

Every effort has been made to provide accurate information in this publication, but changes are inevitable. The publisher cannot be responsible for any resulting loss, inconvenience or injury. We would appreciate it if readers would call our attention to any errors or outdated information by contacting Berlitz Publishing, PO Box 7910, London SE1 1WE, England.
Fax: (44) 20 7403 0290;
e-mail: berlitz@apaguide.co.uk
www.berlitzpublishing.com

© 2006 Apa Publications GmbH & Co.
Verlag KG, Singapore Branch, Singapore

Printed in Singapore by Insight Print Services (Pte) Ltd, 38 Joo Koon Road, Singapore 628990.
Tel: (65) 6865-1600. Fax: (65) 6861-6438
Berlitz Trademark Reg. U.S. Patent Office and other countries. Marca Registrada

➤ Perched on a cliff overlooking the Caribbean, Tulum (page 47) is the most beautifully situated of all the Maya sites

With its great beaches and cosmopolitan atmosphere, Playa del Carmen (page 44) is the top tourist town along the Riviera Maya ▲

◀ Mérida (page 62) is full of colonial treasures and has a vibrant cultural scene

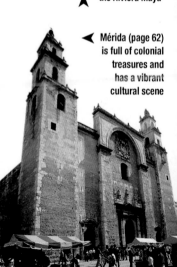

TOP TEN ATTRACTIONS

Cozumel (page 35) has some of the world's best diving among its coral reefs ▼

◀ Xcaret (page 45), an ecopark *par excellence*, has everything from an underground river to Maya ball games

The many attractions of Isla Mujeres (page 32) include snorkeling and diving tours, and spending the day on the glorious Playa Norte beach ▶

The great Maya city of Chichén Itzá (page 53) has as its focal point the magnificent Kukulcán Pyramid ▼

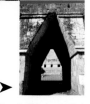

▶ Maya builders excelled themselves in the creation of Uxmal (page 72)

In Cancún (page 25) days are best spent relaxing on the beach ▶

Hidden Worlds (page 47) is the place to go to explore the magical world of flooded caverns and *cenotes* ▶

CONTENTS

Fact Sheets

INTRODUCTION

In 1969, Cancún was a pristine, sandy island washed by the waves of the Caribbean Sea. A sublime 21-km (13-mile) long beach fringed its eastern edge. Its west coast bounded a clear, shallow lagoon carpeted in mangrove, supporting a myriad of wading birds, iguanas, turtles, and other wild creatures. There was little sign of human activity. The footprints of a sophisticated ancient people who had once called this place home had been washed away nearly 500 years before. At 2,000km (1,250 miles) from Mexico City it was so far away that it might never have merited a second thought.

But Mexico had begun to invest in tourism in the late 1960s, and the government was looking for a prime site to develop. Cancún was the perfect location for the world's finest multipurpose super-resort: The temperature rarely drops below 24°C (75°F) and it takes only a few hours to fly to the area from the US, Canada, and other cities in Mexico. Work began in 1970, and today Cancún is one of *the* foremost tourist playgrounds. Its shiny, smart hotels with air-conditioning, room service, and satellite TV cater to nearly 3 million visitors each year; its airport is the second busiest in Mexico. The birds and iguanas can still be found, but they share their habitats with thousands of people who migrate from the snowy, damp northern climes for a few days of R-and-R in this perfect environment. Almost everybody speaks English, and the US dollar can be used as easily as Mexico's currency, the peso.

Water Features
Cancún sits just off the northeastern coast of the Yucatán Peninsula, a finger of land bordering the southern rim of the Gulf of Mexico. The peninsula sits directly south of

Louisiana and Mississippi, north of Belize and Guatemala, west of Cuba, and comprises the Mexican states of Yucatán, Quintana Roo, and Campeche. It is a flat, limestone environment with little surface soil. Water has eroded its surface over millions of years to create hundreds of water-filled caves (cenotes) and watercourses. The surface is capped by a dense tangle of low jungle, home to deer, boar, and jaguar. This lack of soil means that little sediment leaches from the land into the surrounding seas, leaving the water crystal-clear, and either the deep blue of lapis lazuli or, around the shallows, a perfect aquamarine.

Though the landscape can be said to be a little monotonous, beneath the waves you'll find one of the most varied and active marine environments in the whole world. A coral reef, part of the Mesoamerican Reef (the second largest reef system in the

Cenotes

As far as geology is concerned, the really interesting features of the landscape lie beneath the surface. Acting like a giant sponge, with no surface drainage except along the southern border, the Yucatán is riddled with cave systems and sinkholes. Some of the caverns are dramatic, with superb stalactite and stalagmite formations. The sinkholes are the result of the roof of an underground cavern collapsing. Known locally as cenotes (corrupted from the Maya word dzonot by the Spanish), these are and always have been a major source of water for the local inhabitants; indeed the traditional settlement pattern was based on the existence of cenotes. In ancient times, the waters from the sinkholes were held to be sacred; at some cenotes within archaeological sites, vestiges of ancient pottery and human remains indicate that they may have been used for religious sacrificial rites. Today locals and visitors alike use them as swimming pools, or even for diving and snorkeling.

world), runs south of Cancún all along the Caribbean coast of Yucatán. The reef plays host to a permanent population of dozens of species of tropical fish darting fitfully around the polyps, and is regularly visited by numerous denizens of the deep, who use it as a pit-stop along their migration routes.

Colors of the reef

Cozumel, farther offshore south of Cancún and once a pirate stronghold, sits on this reef, making it a natural attraction for divers and snorkelers. Its southern seaboard, made famous by diving pioneer Jacques Cousteau in his early marine films, is now protected under the auspices of the national park service.

The Land of the Maya

Cancún and Cozumel between them seem to have just about everything the fun-loving vacationer could want. Sun all day, warm sea and pale golden sand, diving and snorkeling, watersports in abundance, golf and tennis for those who enjoy a contest, and swim-up bars for those who don't. After dark, hundreds of margaritas or tequila sunrises are served each night before dinner or a dance show.

However, there are attractions here much older than our 21st-century pleasure palaces. In this land of few hills, the jungle betrays evidence of a great civilization – their buildings rise majestically above the tree-tops at sites all across the peninsula. The land of Mexico has seen the rise and fall of a number of great Mesoamerican civilizations.

In the Yucatán, the Maya reigned from around 1500BC to the coming of the Spanish in the 16th century. The Maya have held a fascination for us since the first explorers found evidence of the sophistication of their society. Their calendar was more accurate than ours, they kept time, they were skilled in the use of medicine and surgical techniques, and they could build immense structures over 50m (165ft) high without the use of the wheel or pack animals. Yet when the Spanish came, the Maya were already in decline. Their knowledge seemed to have vanished with the disappearance of a few of their highest caste. We still don't have all the answers to why the civilization declined as it did, and tragically, soon after the Spanish arrived, their priests – in the frenzy of the Inquisition – made huge bonfires of the precious Maya manuscripts. Their secrets, coded on the parchments, simply went up in flames.

The Pyramid of the Magician at Uxmal

The Spanish established their own towns in the Yucatán, often over the ruins of old Maya settlements; today pastel stucco walls, wrought-iron balconies, and geraniums in terracotta pots still give a feel of Castille, Leon, or Madrid. Chief among them is Mérida, a beautiful city of shady plazas, handsome haciendas, and horse-drawn *calesas*.

Today, Maya sites all across the Yucatán are still being excavated and restored. Chichén Itzá – the diamond in an array of Maya gems – is only 2 hours from Cancún, and several other important cities are within traveling distance. While their ancient edifices are being rediscovered, the Maya people have been living in the countryside all along. Most are

Maya children today

farmers, as their ancestors were, planting, harvesting, and taking their goods to market. Their dark eyes, high cheekbones, and diminutive frames bespeak their background. Their first language is often Maya – though of course Spanish is spoken by everyone except the elderly.

Some Maya have moved to Cancún, to make a living from tourism. They have been joined by thousands of others from all across Mexico who have settled here, spawning a worker's city on land that was barren only 30 years ago. Work is plentiful and the life is good – at least for now – as Cancún booms.

Cancún and Cozumel are made for pleasure: for the absolute bliss of doing nothing, or at least just what you feel like doing. No one would blame you for simply sitting by the pool, basking in the sun. Yet to do that would be to miss the other facets of what the region has to offer: beautiful natural wilderness, the majesty of the Maya archaeological sites, pretty Spanish colonial towns, and happy, welcoming people. Enjoy the hedonistic pleasure of resort life. But peek over your sunglasses occasionally. There's a lot worth exploring.

A BRIEF HISTORY

During the last 50 years, a great deal of research has been undertaken to discover more about the great ancient societies of the Yucatán. Huge sections of their daily lives (and particularly the reason they came to abandon their cities) are still shrouded in mystery, but great strides have been made in deciphering their hieroglyphs and stelae (inscribed stone pillars). Despite these mysteries, there are few places in the world where the past feels as close as it does in the Yucatán. The thatched huts *(na)* that appear in 1,000-year-old carvings at

Uxmal can be seen today in every roadside village. The stone *metates*, or grinding dishes, that grace many a kitchen in town or village, are identical to those left as offerings to the rain gods in centuries past. Away from the cities, the people still speak the Maya tongue, and their religious beliefs still bear the imprint of the ancient rituals of their ancestors.

The Maya thatched hut or *na*, still a feature of the Yucatán

The Maya

The Maya's ancestors arrived in Central America many thousands of years ago. Small bands of Asiatic hunters migrated across the Bering Strait land bridge before 12,000BC and gradually spread southward through the Americas. During the Archaic period (after 5,200BC), these people settled in what is now modern Mexico. They developed a primitive agriculture, domesticating cattle and cultivating corn, beans, chili peppers, and squash (a pumpkin-like vegetable) in burned clearings in the jungle. Over time, a society developed that was so successful they could devote time to activities other than simple food cultivation. These people, known as the Olmec, are considered to be the first Mesoamerican culture, the one from which all others evolved. They developed a calendar based on a 52-year cycle, and also constructed pyramids for worship.

By 1500BC the group that came to be known as the Maya settled in an area that stretched from the Pacific coast to the southern Yucatán, taking in modern-day Guatemala, Belize, the western parts of El Salvador and Honduras, and the Mexican state of Campeche. In the succeeding centuries they migrated into the northern Yucatán – an area that now forms the modern Mexican states of Yucatán, Quintana Roo, and the northern part of Campeche.

Though their antecedents are still shadowy, they were much influenced by the Olmec. They developed and refined the Olmec calendar and counting system, and improved their building practices. The whole Yucatán Peninsula witnessed

The Maya Calendars

Over the centuries, the Maya developed two different but interrelated calendar systems. The Maya Round Calendar consisted of 20 named days that interlocked like a cogwheel with the numbers one to 13, giving a total cycle of 260 days. Alongside this system was one more closely based on the sun's movement, with 18 months each 20 days long and a further five days at the end to complete the solar cycle of 365 days. These two calendar systems came back to their starting point every 18,980 days, or 52 years, signifying a rebirth. Interestingly, every 52 years was the frequency with which the Maya added a new layer to their temple-pyramids.

Artifacts in the Balancanché caves near Chichén Itzá

the flowering of classic Maya civilization and a society of great sophistication; with its magnificent pyramids, temples, and palaces decorated with wall paintings and carved low-reliefs, a written language of hieroglyphics, and complicated medical procedures to heal the injured or the sick. Maya astronomers tracked the movements of the heavenly bodies, predicting eclipses and marking the times for the planting of the new corn. In fact, corn came to symbolize life for the Maya – in their myths of creation, mankind was formed from lumps of maize dough. Elaborate rituals grew up around the preparation of the *milpas* (cornfields) and the planting and harvesting of the crop whose success depended on the coming of the annual rains. These rituals were undertaken by a small number of initiates who controlled the knowledge of the Maya. Because the region has no surface rivers, rain was a precious resource and the Maya saw any stock of water, such as the limestone water holes, or *cenotes,* as holy places. The rain god Chaac was a very important deity, whose image can be seen at every Maya site.

But there was a dark side to this sophisticated society. The Maya viewed their gods not as benevolent guides but as changeable spirits in need of constant appeasement. To incur the wrath of the gods would result in drought, a loss of crops, and certain starvation. To keep the gods happy, the people offered sacrifices at their great pyramid temples in ceremonies overseen by a powerful caste of high priests. Grain and animals were used, but the gods came to demand more, and a cult of human sacrifice grew. The Maya went out on raiding parties, taking hostages from the surrounding lands to use in their bloody ceremonies. The murals and reliefs at Maya cities tell gory tales of beheading and the tearing out of human hearts to appease the lords of the underworld. Archaeologists dredging the Sacred Cenote of Chichén Itzá recovered dozens of human skeletons, thought to be the remains of victims sacrificed to the rain god.

Maya civilization in the northern Yucatán reached its peak around AD900–1200, but for reasons still unknown – perhaps civil war, drought, or disease – the great cities were abandoned. By the time the Spaniards arrived in the early 16th century the jungle was reclaiming the pyramids; the richly painted murals of warriors, Maya lords, animals, and gods

Frederick Catherwood's famous depiction of the Arch of Labná

were already crumbling and dissolving in the warm rain. The priest caste seemed to have vanished, along with their knowledge. The only people the Spanish found were farmers.

In the Wake of Cortés

The first recorded Europeans to arrive in the Yucatán, in 1511, were doubly unfortunate: a group of Spanish sailors survived a shipwreck on the coast of what is now Quintana Roo, only to be sacrificed by the Maya natives. However, two of them were allowed to live as slaves and one, Gonzalo Guerrero, went native and married the chief's daughter. His children were the first *mestizos* – the people of mixed Indian and Spanish blood who now make up 55 percent of the Mexican population.

In 1517, an expedition led by Francisco Hernandez de Cordobá landed on the west coast of the Yucatán, near Campeche, but was beaten back by a hail of arrows from the hostile natives. However, the following year ambitious young Captain Juan de Grijalva discovered the island of Cozumel and skirted the coast of the peninsula, hearing tales from the Indians of the great civilization of the Aztecs. Here, they told him, you can find a city made of gold.

How Yucatán Got Its Name

One story claims that the captain of one of the first Spanish ships to reach the peninsula went ashore and was met by a delegation of Indians. The captain asked the chief (in Spanish of course) 'What land is this?' and the Indian's answer was '*Ci u than,*' which meant 'I do not understand your words' in the native language. The captain heard this as '*Yucatán,*' and so the name stuck. Another theory says that the name comes from the local Yucca plant, plus *tal* or *hale*, which means the heap of earth in which the plant grows.

Grijalva's stories focused Spanish attention on central Mexico, and in 1519 Hernan Cortés landed in Veracruz, to embark on an expedition that would end in the conquest of Moctezuma and the Aztec Empire. Though he had begun his campaign without the King's authority, once news of the treasures captured by Cortés reached Madrid, a royal warrant was dispatched to legitimize the victory and create 'New Spain' – the latest Spanish colony. However, it was left

Francisco de Montejo, founder of modern Mérida

to Don Francisco de Montejo, 'a gentleman of Seville,' following in the great conquistador's wake, to take possession of the Yucatán in the name of the Spanish king.

Arriving on the coast in 1527, Montejo's forces were hindered by the dense jungle and withering climate, and were met by fierce resistance from the natives. To make matters worse, news of great riches discovered in Peru led many of his men to desert in search of greater rewards. The campaign went so badly that by 1535 the Spaniards had been completely driven out of the Yucatán.

In 1537 another force, under the command of Montejo el Mozo (the Younger), Don Francisco's son, set out to plant the Spanish standard on Yucatecan soil. At first ill fortune dogged them; the dwindling force was besieged in Champotón, on the west coast, for two miserable years. With reinforcements, the Spaniards managed to establish a beachhead. A band of only 57 men, led by Montejo el Mozo's cousin (yet another Don

Francisco), marched inland to take the Maya village of T'Ho. The Indians gathered their forces for one last great battle, and thousands of them fell upon the Spanish camp, now defended by 200 men. The horses and superior weaponry of the Spaniards gave them the edge, and they slaughtered hundreds of Indian warriors. After the battle, local chiefs made peace with the invaders and, on January 6 1542, the Montejos founded the Spanish city of Mérida on the site.

The Caste War

In July 1562, in the Yucatán village of Maní, Bishop Diego de Landa gathered together hundreds of 'idols' and all he could find of the Maya scriptures and publicly burned them in front of the church of San Miguel Arcángel, thereby destroying virtually all Maya recorded history in a single night.

Under Spanish rule, land was taken from the Maya and turned over to tobacco and sugarcane plantations, and the once-proud Indians were reduced to farm laborers. Franciscan friars, such as the 16th-century Bishop Diego de Landa, were dispatched from Europe to spread the Christian faith throughout the peninsula, though they met with some resistance – any similarity between the early Yucatecan churches and military fortresses is not accidental. Eventually, the Maya accepted the new faith, but combined it with elements of their old beliefs. Unfortunately, the Spanish were over zealous, and many chronicles relating to Maya beliefs and culture were destroyed (see panel).

In 1821, Mexico declared its independence from Spain. Tension had been simmering for decades, fostered by Spain's treatment of her New-Spanish-born colonists, or *criollos* (deemed to be second-class citizens compared to those born in the homeland). Her trade laws decreed that everything produced in New Spain must first cross the

Atlantic to Spain before being traded with a third country so that the proper taxes and tariffs could be collected. The geography of the northern Yucatán region separated it physically from the rest of New Spain, and fewer colonial landowners settled here than the area around the new capital (now Mexico City). Furthermore, this isolation led to the development of a strong independent streak for both colonists and indigenous peoples. The Yucatán declared its independence in 1821 but did not join the fledgling country of Mexico until 1823. In 1840, it changed its mind, and withdrew from the union. This was the catalyst for the Maya to take up arms against their colonial oppressors.

In 1847, a savage uprising known as the Caste War saw Maya rebels massacre white settlers and take control of nearly two-thirds of the peninsula. By 1850 they had driven the Mexicans back to their strongholds in Mérida and Campeche. However, in an amazing turnaround, the Maya's ancient beliefs became their undoing. Just when the Mexicans were on the point of surrender, the rains came early and the Indians, obedient to their gods, dropped their weapons and returned to their *milpas* to plant the sacred corn. The settlers called in reinforcements and wreaked a terrible revenge on the natives. One group of rebels, known as the Chan Santa Cruz, held out in the jungles of Quintana Roo around the city of Tulum, harrying the Mexicans and making the east coast of the Yucatán a dangerous area, off-limits until well into the 20th century.

The church in Maní where the Maya books were burned

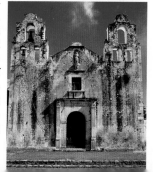

The Henequen Boom

The henequen plant

Life was hard in the northern Yucatán, as the lack of surface water and the limestone sub-surface made it difficult to grow commercial crops or raise cattle. However, in the late 19th century, the hacienda, or plantation owners found a crop that grew successfully and was much in demand around the world – the henequen plant. The fibers produced by henequen could be made into rope and twine, indispensable for seafaring and international trade. Yucatán was the principal producer, exporting their goods through the port of Sisal on the northern coast. Processed henequen soon became known around the world as sisal.

The money earned by the plantation owners was spent on grand mansions along Mérida's Paseo de Montejo; they were filled with the best in furniture, porcelain, and artwork. The Indians, however, worked the land for a pittance. In the east, some scraped out a living by tapping the sap of the zapote or chicle tree and selling it to American manufacturers of chewing gum. Unfortunately, when the henequen bubble burst in the 1930s with the advent of synthetic fibers, the peninsula fell into an economic decline from which there seemed to be little hope of respite.

Meanwhile, under the presidency of Porfirio Diaz, Quintana Roo on the Yucatán peninsula's eastern coast – named after Andreas Quintana Roo, a writer and independence movement leader between 1810 and 1821 – was declared a territory of Mexico in 1902. Government troops clamped down on rebellious Indians, who continued to resist until a peace treaty was finally negotiated in 1935. The overthrow of Porfirio Diaz in 1917 led to reform and a new constitution, including a bill of rights for Mexican workers. At the instigation of local socialist leader Felipe Carillo Puerto (assassinated in 1924), many haciendas were broken up and returned to the people. But the Yucatán remained a backwater, largely forgotten and ignored. No overland route existed from Mérida to the rest of Mexico until 1949, when the first railroad arrived. Before then, all commercial travel to and from the peninsula was by sea.

Mexico's Mega-Resort

On the beach at Cancún

Despite its considerable oil reserves and mineral wealth, debt, booming population growth, and grinding poverty have crippled the economy of modern Mexico. In an effort to bring more hard currency into the country, the government decided to promote tourism. A 3-year study of various sites was conducted by a consortium of government and private interests, and the deserted island of Cancún won out: not only was it a beautiful spot, but its use would revive the flagging economy of the Yucatán and finally bring Quintana Roo into the fold. The territory was eventually granted statehood in 1974, the same year that Cancún opened to the public.

Cancún is now Mexico's most popular holiday destination, pulling in almost 3 million tourists each year. New roads have appeared, and televisions and refrigerators are now the norm in villages that didn't even have electricity 20 years ago. Despite creating a pocket of wealth for the region, Mexico itself suffered a number of crises in the 1980s and 1990s, including a drastic devaluation of the peso in 1995 following months of economic chaos. Economic progress has often been hampered by political corruption, but the election of Vincente Fox of the National Action Party as the country's president in 2000 has given the people new hope that their voice will be heard after decades of often autocratic, single-party rule.

Beyond all the economic and political challenges, a pressing question for the Yucatán itself is whether development can be controlled. What was a deserted coastline three decades ago is now a bustling Riviera. Coral reefs are being damaged by careless divers; lagoons that once teemed with tropical fish are now being polluted by suntan lotion; the beaches where sea turtles once laid their eggs are being taken over by sun-beds and volleyball nets and turtles that once cruised the coastal waters are now an endangered species. Conservation areas such as Río Lagartos, in the north, give hope for the future, but the battle between the conflicting demands of development and conservation is set to continue.

Egret in the mangroves of Río Lagartos

Historical Landmarks

circa 1500BC The Maya settle in the Yucatán.

AD300–900 The classic period of Maya civilization, during which its finest structures are erected across the region, including those at Uxmal, Cobá, and Chichén Itzá (Old Chichén).

1200–1500 Decline of the Maya civilization, cities abandoned and knowledge lost.

1511 Spanish sailors land in the Yucatán.

1519 Cortés lands on mainland Mexico, declaring it to be New Spain.

1542 The city of Mérida is founded by Spanish colonists.

1562 Maya manuscripts are assembled and burned at Maní.

1821 Mexico declares independence.

1840 Yucatán State declares itself independent of Mexico.

1847–1848 The Caste War; the Maya launch an unsuccessful attack on colonial landowners.

1850–1900 The planting of henequen results in a boom that brings wealth to Yucatán landowners.

1902 Quintana Roo becomes a territory of Mexico.

1917 Porfirio Diaz overthrown; a new Mexican constitution includes a Bill of Worker's Rights.

1923 First reconstruction work undertaken in Chichén Itzá.

1949 A railroad track provides the first overland route linking Mérida to Mexico City.

1974 Cancún resort opens to the public, Quintana Roo becomes a state of Mexico.

1993 Mexico signs the North American Free Trade Agreement (NAFTA) with the US and Canada.

1997 A new cruise port is built across the coral reef along Cozumel's western shoreline.

2000 Vicente Fox is elected Mexican president. The city of Mérida celebrates a year as the 'Continental Capital of Culture'.

2005 In October, Hurricane Wilma hits the coast of the Yucatán, causing considerable damage to the local infrastructure.

WHERE TO GO

CANCÚN

When the Mexican government decided to improve its economy by developing its tourist industry, a totally new, tailor-made, high-class resort was the aim; the major decision was where its site should be. Many factors were taken into account before a short list of locations was entered into a computer. When the final results were correlated, Cancún was top of the list.

This location had many natural attributes in its favor. Twenty-seven kilometers (17 miles) long and less than a kilometer wide, the island is shaped like the number seven, and separated from the Yucatán peninsula by only 10m (33ft) of water. Its eastern shoreline is one **long beach** of fine white sand (there are seven named beaches along the strip), which is washed by the translucent azure waters of the Caribbean. Between the island and the mainland is **Laguna Nichupté**, a huge seawater lagoon bounded by mangrove swamps that are havens to numerous species of wildlife.

Today a string of hotels has taken much of the beachfront real estate; the balance given over to bars, nightclubs, and shopping malls. On the lagoon side, watersports and eco-tours abound in the calmer shallow waters. Blue signs denote public beach access and there are no restrictions, so you can walk the island's full length without concerns about trespass. All in all, Cancún has everything needed for the perfect relaxing vacation.

Finding your way around the resort couldn't be simpler. There is only one main thoroughfare, **Kukulcán Boulevard**, running the full length of the island, and every hotel and attraction is only a few strides from it. The addresses of most

Whether you work on your tan or lounge beneath the *palapas*, days in Cancún are best spent on the beach

hotels or restaurants will include their position on Kukulcán Boulevard in kilometers; the farther south, the bigger the number. This guide explores the island from north to south, giving the exact location of attractions in kilometers to make it easy for you to find what you need. You could rent a vehicle of some sort to travel back and forth to your hotel, but there is a very reliable and inexpensive bus service stopping regularly, and usually directly outside the major hotels, at intervals along the route. The buses run from early morning to midnight.

Hotel Zone

Crossing from the mainland onto the island – into the area called the Hotel Zone – the lagoon with its rich mangrove forest is on the right. You may see a passing pleasure-boat on the water, or a jet-ski convoy on the lookout for wildlife such as herons, pelicans, deer, wild boar, even the occasional crocodile – though the local creatures tend to only be found only in the most remote parts of the mangrove, well away from humans.

This part of Cancún has the calmest sea for swimming and snorkeling, lying as it does in the shelter of Isla Mujeres just offshore. At km 3.5, just before the causeway over to the island, you'll find **Playa Linda Marine Terminal**, where a number of pleasure craft leave for trips to Isla Mujeres or sunset cruises. One, the *Captain Hook*, resembles a pirate ship; shipmates play games while sailing the high seas. This is also the location of the **El Embarcadero** complex, whose attractions include the fascinating **Museo de Arte Popular Mexicano**, with its colorful array of local folk art, and the **Torre Escénica**, a revolving observation tower offering great views. On Tuesdays and Fridays you can also see music and dance spectaculars performed at the **Teatro de Cancún**.

At km 5 you will pass a huge Mexican flag, one of only seven this size in the whole country. You can see it from most points on the island; it is only taken down in high winds. Just beyond the flag on the left is **Tortuga Pier**, hosting boating trips and the ferry terminal, plus access to **Playa Tortuga** beach. Kilometer 7 sees a right turn to the 18-hole **Pok-Ta-Pok** golf course, which is located on a large landmass that juts out into the lagoon.

Punta Cancún, the area around km 8.5, where the island bends south, forms the heart of the Hotel Zone,

Nights can be spent in discos such as Coco Bongo

the focus for activity of all kinds. A number of shopping malls can be found here, including **Plaza Caracol**, a mix of craft and tourist stores; **Mayafair**, with its unmistakable facade fashioned of Chaac masks; and **Forum by the Sea**, with several fast-food eateries and a cine-complex showing the latest Hollywood movies. Dominating the scene here is the **Centro de Convenciones** (Convention Center), which hosts musical and artistic exhibitions: check the program during your visit. Near the main entrance is the **Museo Arqueológico de Cancún** (Cancún Archaeological Museum; open daily 9am–8pm; admission fee), displaying pottery, masks, and jewelry from the El Rey site and others in Quintana Roo.

South of the Convention Center is the Hotel Zone craft market – designated the Flea Market on the sign outside. Prices for crafts and knickknacks in this warren of stands are negotiable, and generally lower than in the malls.

Kilometers 11 to 13 have three more shopping malls. On the lagoon side, the first is **Flamingo Plaza**; a bit farther south is **La Isla Shopping Village**, fashioned after a Venetian lagoon. This development boasts several restaurants, a nightclub and movie-theater complex. Children will enjoy Maya Ventura, a gigantic maze that lets them explore the Maya world with the help of a special electronic key; and at the Interactive Aquarium visitors can have a close-up look at tropical fish, feed the sharks or go swimming with dolphins. **Plaza Kukulcán**, at km 13 on the ocean side, has outlets for designer clothing,

Taxis are very expensive in Cancún, particularly for travel within the Hotel Zone. So the best and cheapest way of getting around is by bus. Regular buses ply between the Hotel Zone and downtown, and they cost just a few pesos a ride. They stop outside all the major shopping and recreation centers and the main hotels.

An excursion into the lagoon with AquaWorld

jewelry, and accessories, plus fine dining, a movie-theater, and a bowling complex. The large interior spaces are used for regular art exhibitions.

At km 15.2, on the lagoon side, is **AquaWorld**, which sells and rents just about every piece of equipment you need to travel on, under, or above the water; it is also one of the largest accredited diving instruction centers in Mexico. Head out into the lagoon on one of the fleets of jet-skis or small power boats, sign up for a snorkeling tour, or if you'd like to see marine life but stay dry, ride the *Sub See Explorer*, a mini-submarine with viewing windows so you get just as good a view as those in wet suits. If you still have the energy, AquaWorld offers Skyrider, a two-seat para-chair that floats in the sky across the lagoon.

Kilometer 18 is the location of the only public Maya site in the Cancún region (there are small pyramids located in the ground of the Pyramides Hotel, but these are not accessible to

Ruinas del Rey, with the Hilton Hotel in the background

non-guests). The **Ruinas del Rey** (King's Ruins; open daily 8am–5pm; admission fee) are set in low jungle, and bounded on the lagoon side by the greens of the Hilton Cancún Beach and Golf Resort. An occasional stray ball is found within the archaeological site; guides will joke that it was the Maya, not the Scots, who invented the game. The El Rey buildings are not large by Maya standards. The temples were built in line rather than in a cluster, with the largest in the middle. Lizards about half a meter (2ft) long call the walls home, basking in the sunshine but disappearing in a flash if you venture too close. Opposite the entrance to the ruins is access to the most southerly beach on the main strip, Playa Delphines.

Toward the very bottom of the island, at km 21, is **Punta Nizuc**. The land in this area is mostly mangrove swamp and a haven for wildlife, being remote from the tourist activity of the Hotel Zone. But when you reach km 25, you'll find **Parque Nizuc**, a commercial water park featuring 'Wet'n-Wild' water slides, wave pool, and river rides, with a sandy beach and lagoon area to enjoy.

Downtown Cancún

The Cancún Hotel Zone needs a vast number of support workers both for hotel service and continued development. Most of them live in **El Centro**, the downtown part of Cancún on the mainland just a few kilometers away, an area that was developed concurrently with the Hotel Zone. It is considered a pleasant place to live by the people who travel from all over Mexico to work in the resort. A series of service industries thrive, along with a lower-key tourist sector.

Downtown Cancún, built on a grid plan, is dominated by **Avenida Tulum**, which runs north–south through the town. Here you will find stores, restaurants, currency exchange offices, and travel agents. **Avenida Cobá** leads from the Hotel Zone into town; most of the important buildings on Avenida Tulum can be found to the north of Cobá. Firstly, the offices of the **Cancún Convention and Visitors Bureau** are on the corner of Cobá and Tulum. Heading north, at **Hi-Kuic craft market** you'll find the same goods as in the Hotel Zone, but prices are a little lower. Following are the police station and Ayuntamiento Benito Juárez, the city hall. The traffic circle at the top of this block (Tulum and Uxmal) has a distinctive sculpture as its centerpiece, featuring carvings depicting the eras of Mexico's history. Just beyond this is the bus station, where regular services depart west to Mérida and south along the Riviera Maya to Tulum.

A block west of Avenida Tulum is **Avenida Yaxchilán**, where you'll find the main post office. Between the two is Parque de las Palapas, a small park and open-air concert pavilion, where local families meet to talk, listen to live music, and while the evenings away. On the streets around the park – each named after a flower – there are small hotels and restaurants, plus stands selling fresh juices or hot snacks.

A good spot to check out souvenirs is Mercado Veinteocho (Market 28). Just off Avenida Yaxchilán and Sunyaxchen, this popular market is filled with stores selling many of the same souvenir items found in the Hotel Zone, but at half the price.

Avenida Tulum leads north, and then veers east to **Puerto Juárez**, the port for passenger ferries to Isla Mujeres. These depart every half hour during the daytime, with both locals and visitors aboard.

ISLA MUJERES

Isla Mujeres (Island of the Women) lies only 8km (5 miles) offshore from Cancún; the 20-minute ferry ride transports you from an ultra-modern atmosphere to an environment in which time seems to move more slowly. Several companies offer one-day sailing trips to Isla Mujeres, often including lunch and snorkeling; they depart from Playa Linda and Pier Tortugas in the Hotel Zone.

Isla Mujeres now has a population of around 15,000. In past centuries, however, it was the haunt of Caribbean pirates, being far from the clutches of colonial overlords in

The waterfront at Isla Mujeres

Havana, San Juan in Puerto Rico, and Panama City, the nearest colonial outposts. The first European to arrive was Spanish explorer Francisco Hernández de Córdoba, who landed in 1517 and discovered a number of small temples built for the fertility goddess Ix-chel. It was he who named the island. Isla Mujeres is no more than 8km (5 miles) in length, less than a kilometer (½ mile) at its widest point, and split by inland lakes and bays. One main road forms an ellipse, following the shape of the coastline.

Most ferries deposit you at the north of the island, on the main pier of the only town on Mujeres. Craft stores and bars crowd onto the sidewalks and paved streets. The place bustles, especially when the ferries arrive. As afternoon turns to evening and the day-trippers head back to Cancún, Isla Mujeres takes on a much quieter character. The island has many loyal fans who return year after year for its particular atmosphere.

Island Highlights

A few minutes' walk north of town is **Playa Norte**. With its shallow, sheltered waters and fine white sand, this is a real paradise beach; the best time to get there is early in the morning before the crowds arrive, when you can pick your spot under a coconut palm.

Heading south out of town you'll pass the Mexican naval base and a small commercial airstrip before traveling alongside **Laguna Makax** on the right. Sheltered from the Caribbean Sea by the island itself, it has for centuries been a safe harbor during storms and hurricanes. Pirate fleets stopped here, because passing naval vessels would not see their ships.

On the far side of Laguna Mekax is **Tortugranja** (Turtle Farm; open daily 9am–5pm; admission fee), which has played a major role in protecting six species of the endangered marine creatures and trying to build their numbers. Every year, nest sites are protected and a number of eggs removed. The hatchlings are cared for until they are a year old, and then returned to the ocean. You can see the young turtles throughout the year, but the best time to visit the farm is during egg-laying season; from May through September.

Farther south, near Playa Lancheros, is the **Hacienda Mundaca** (admission fee) once the property of one of the island's most colorful characters, the pirate and slave trader Fermin Mundaca de Marechaja. He retired to Isla Mujeres in 1858, and his hacienda once covered more than a third of the island. He dedicated it to a local girl with whom he had fallen in love and who he called *La Triguena* (the brunette); she was 18 years old at the time (37 years his junior), and so infatuated was he that he had her name carved into the entrance arches of his hacienda. But the brunette spurned his affections, and married a local man instead. The hacienda's remaining structures and gardens have been restored and a small

Turtle Farm resident

zoo has been added. You will see monkeys, various birds, crocodiles, pythons, and even a jaguar.

At the southern tip of the island is the **Garrafón-Punta Sur National Park**, encompassing a rocky headland that plunges down into the great Mesoamerican Reef. On the cliff top at Punta Sur, beyond the lighthouse, stand the ruins of a Maya temple dedicated to Ix-chel, the fertility goddess, and equipped with observation points that were used to make astronomical observations. Just to the north of Punta Sur, on the west side, is the **Garrafón Marine Park**, which has been developed to provide facilities for divers and snorkelers. The shallow waters above the reef here are particularly suited to novice snorkelers; divers and snorkelers can also take a boat excursion to the main reef off Punta Sur.

A bronze cross, almost 12m (39ft) high, weighing 1 tonne, was mounted in the sea between the island and the mainland near the Manchones Reef in 1994. The Cross of the Bay is a tribute to the men and women who have lost their lives at sea. Thousands of divers participate in a 'mass dive' here on August 17 each year.

COZUMEL

Cozumel was brought to the world's attention by Jacques Cousteau's diving films of the 1960s. With the second-longest coral reef in the world just off its western coastline, it soon became a haunt for all those who enjoyed the underwater world. Today, along with enjoying status as one of the premier dive islands in the world, it is also a duty-free cruise port, with shopping to match the best in the Caribbean.

However, Cozumel has a much longer history of human habitation. It was a Maya site of some importance, being the center of worship for the fertility goddess Ix-chel. Cozumel became a destination for Maya pilgrims from all over the Yucatán throughout the post-classic period (AD900–1530). The Maya who lived here traded salt and honey all along the coast; Xcaret was their major port on the mainland.

The Spanish conducted the first Catholic Mass in Mexico here after their arrival in 1518, but they had little interest in the island. It remained almost uninhabited through the 18th century. But following the War of the Castes in 1847–48, several rebel families settled here to escape retribution by colonial landowners on the Yucatecan mainland. They eked out a simple living for decades until the invention of the scuba tank. And the rest, as they say, is history.

Cozumel has multiple personalities; it caters to divers who go to bed early and rise with the sun, yet it also has occasionally raucous nightlife for those who want to stay out and party. Those who know the island well refer to this phenom-

The reason many people come to Cozumel

enon as the 'wet' side and the 'dry' side. Day-trippers who arrive on their huge cruise ships – or on daily ferries from Playa del Carmen – add an extra dimension; they want to see everything in a few hours, so the slow routine of island life speeds up considerably when they arrive.

Relaxing in San Miguel

San Miguel

There is only one major settlement on Cozumel, the capital, **San Miguel de Cozumel**; it's a bustling town chock-full of souvenir stores, duty-free emporiums, bars, and assorted cafés and restaurants. If you arrive on the island by ferry from the mainland, you'll be dropped off directly opposite the heart of the downtown area, **Plaza del Sol**, also called the *zócalo*. This large, tree-lined square is where everyone meets for coffee, or lunch at one of the cafés nearby. Several streets surrounding the square are traffic-free, and you can stroll at your leisure among the stores selling T-shirts, pottery, onyx, and silver. The storeowners have a practiced line and can be pretty persuasive, so it pays to have a sense of humor – or a few words of Spanish so you can join in the banter.

The street running along the seafront is **Avenida Rafael Melgar**, also known as the Malecón, almost constantly busy with traffic. It is lined with numerous duty-free stores selling fragrances, designer clothing, and jewelry and gemstones. Above these are bars and restaurants that keep the street buzzing until the early hours of the morning. Stop in at the

➤ **Museo de la Isla de Cozumel** (Museum of the Island of Cozumel; open daily 9am–5pm; admission fee) on Avenida Melgar, which displays some interesting artifacts found on the island and salvaged from wrecks around its shores. The two main rooms on the first floor offer simple explanations about the geology of the Yucatán peninsula and the development of coral reefs offshore. The second-floor rooms tell the story of Cozumel's history, from ancient Maya carvings to conquistador helmets and swords. There is also a room dedicated to the families who settled in Cozumel in the 19th century – after the War of the Castes – and who have developed the island since that time.

North of town you will find the airport, with several flights daily to other parts of Mexico and a few cities in the US. Several of the older hotels are located along the road here, though the rocky shoreline has fewer beaches than in the south.

Traveling around Cozumel couldn't be easier. The island is almost encircled by a coastal road, the Costera Sur, and running across the middle, between San Miguel and the east coast, is the Carretera Transversal. The only coastal parts of the island to which access is limited are the northwest and southern tips, both havens for birds and other wildlife. The best way of getting around is by rental car or moped, but it's also possible to take a taxi.

The West Coast

South of San Miguel, you will find the major cruise port at **La Ceiba**, around 3km (2 miles) from town. Several large cruise vessels dock each week, bringing a flurry of activity. There is a good beach at La Ceiba and a number of hotels, plus several dive outfits have bases here – you can book a class or rent equipment. Farther south, in the ocean offshore, the reef holds the attention of even the most experienced divers because of its variety of marine and coral life. Turtles, rays, sharks, and many species of colorful tropical fish can be found here, many at a reasonable depth for novice divers – though the reef walls are better left to those with experience. The booking office for Atlantis Submarine is also here; this mini-submersible is ideal for non-divers, allowing a glimpse of the thriving underwater world without your having to get wet.

Preparations at Cozumel beach Park, Playa del Sol

South of the cruise port, the road leads away from the urban development and out into the countryside. This part of the island has some of the best and most sheltered beaches. In recent years, a number of excellent resort hotels have been built on large plots of land; you will see their gated entrances as you drive by. Next to these are the more modest accommodations that for years have catered to dedicated divers.

Around 5km (3 miles) from town you will find the entrance to **Chankanaab State Park** (open daily 8am–5pm; admission fee). This was one of the first sites on the island to offer organized reef snorkeling in an offshore lagoon, though as it became more popular it developed other attractions. Snorkeling is still extremely good offshore, though the lagoon site is now devoid of marine life and is used simply as a safe swimming area. Chankanaab offers a botanical garden and a sculpture park displaying native art from all areas of Mexico. It has a dive store, beach umbrellas, sun beds, and two restaurants.

> More than 80 percent of Cozumel's reefs are now protected within the Cozumel Reefs National Park, which was created in 1996. There is a small daily charge for diving in the park.

Perhaps the prize of the park goes to the 'Swim with the Dolphins' program. The dolphins are kept in open water just offshore. Small groups of people can enter the water with the dolphins; an instructor controls the activities.

South from Chankanaab you can stop at a number of fine sandy beaches on the west coast. The major sites are **Playa San Francisco**, **Playa del Sol**, and **Playa Palancar**. All the main beaches have public access and each has its own café-bar, watersports facilities, and lockers for beachgoers. The water is a beautiful clear turquoise color; you will see small dive or snorkel boats bobbing offshore as you soak up the sun. These waters offer some of the best diving and snorkeling in the world. The variety of marine life living on and around the coral reef here is amazing, with many of the largest migratory fish species paying a visit at different times of the year.

Between Playa del Sol and Playa Palancar is a dirt road marked by an arch printed with the words El Cedral that veers left from the main highway. The road is poor and it requires some patience to avoid the potholes, but it leads to **El Cedral**, from where it is possible to ride a horse to Maya ruins deep in the forest (take insect repellent if you intend to make the journey). It was at El Cedral that the first Catholic Mass was said in Mexico, on May 6 1518. In May each year the settlement reenacts the event and also holds a fiesta with horseback riding, music, and dancing.

The very southern tip of the island is a national park, protected from the development, which threatened its wild but fragile environment. The **Parque Punta Sur** (South Point Park; open daily 8am–6pm; admission fee) was opened in

1999. Access is not permitted by car, but the park provides electric bicycles, buggies, and a colorful open-sided tour bus to give access to the interior. At the car park an information center provides details about the park and its flora and fauna. Within Punta Sur's 1,100 hectares (2,718 acres) are the coast, with its wild beaches and sand dunes, and the interior lagoons and mangrove swamps, with a population of crocodiles and bird species. You can explore Punta Celerain, the most southerly point of Cozumel and now part of the park, and **Punta Celerain Lighthouse**, once protector of shipping in the area, and now refurbished to house the **Museo de la Navegación** (Navigation Museum). A series of dioramas in both Spanish and English explain navigation methods through the ages, including those of the Maya who lived in the region. One room is dedicated to the lighthouse-keepers and their families.

Punta Celerain Lighthouse

The East Coast

From Punta Sur the main highway heads north up the east coast. The conditions here offer quite a contrast to the west, with the waves of the Caribbean lashing against limestone rocks, and the low vegetation leaning inward, blown by the sea breezes. The whole area has a stark and wild beauty, reminiscent perhaps of the time when Cozumel was the haunt of pirates and renegades. The tidal surge is very strong here, so swimming and snorkeling are not advised. Other than a few farms, there is little development until you reach **Playa Morena**, with its bar and souvenir stand. Here the road makes a sharp left turn to cut across the heart of the island. If you wish to continue north from here (on foot, horseback, or four-wheel-drive vehicle), you will eventually reach the northern lighthouse at **Punta Molas**, having passed the Maya ruins of El Castillo Real along the way. Take the sensible precautions if you make this trip – drinking water, sun protection, insect repellent, and an extra layer of clothing are all advisable.

Across the Middle

The road leading back to San Miguel, called the **Carretera Transversal**, hosts a few souvenir stands where prices may be a little lower than in town – if you're prepared to barter. Six kilometers (4 miles) from Playa Morena is the entrance to the **San Gervasio Archaeological Park** (open daily 7am–4pm; admission fee). The remains of San Gervasio are located some distance from the site entrance, and though not on the scale of the major Maya settlements of the mainland, the beautiful tropical park environment makes the ruins worth exploring. Most structures date from the late post-classic period (1200–1530); the site was still in use when the Spanish arrived. At the **Estructura Manitas** (Little Hands Structure), you can clearly see the red handprints, dating from around 1000, on the inside wall of the temple. From here you can walk the route of a short sacred *sacbé* (Maya road) to the central group of small buildings. One is **El Osario** (Ossuary), where the remains of several Maya were found. Some 500m (⅓ mile) behind here is **Kana Nah** (Tall House), which is one of the largest structures at the site. It was the main temple, where the fertility goddess, Ix-chel, was worshiped.

The ruins of Tulum at the southern end of the Riviera Maya

ALONG THE RIVIERA MAYA TO TULUM

When tourism first came to this area of the Yucatán peninsula, the coastline between Cancún and Tulum was a pristine natural landscape, broken only by a few villages. Rocky coastal inlets where seawater mingles with the freshwater of several *cenotes* are separated by acres of virgin mangrove. Parts of the coastline have sandy beaches that seem as if no human has ever set foot on them.

Of course, with the success of Cancún developers have looked for other opportunities in the region, and this stretch of coastline is gradually being taken for tourist development. Luckily, not every development mimics the grand resorts of Cancún, and there is some variety here, in both style and atmosphere; there are a number of all-inclusive hotel complexes, yet there are also interesting towns and ports. Tulum, with its magnificent Maya ruins, forms a natural southerly point to the strip of coastal development, which has been given the name 'The Riviera Maya.' The area is easy to explore by vehicle, as Highway 307, the main road following the coastline – though in some places a few kilometers inland from it – is in good condition; most of it is now a four-lane highway. There is also an excellent bus service linking the major settlements and large hotels, which takes around 2 hours to run the whole length of the Riviera.

Playa del Carmen

Traveling south from Cancún, the first town you will pass, at 36km (22 miles), is **Puerto Morelos**, the port for vehicle ferries to the island of Cozumel. A 30-minute journey from Cancún is **Tres Ríos**, a natural reserve with facilities for snorkeling, kayaking, and horseback riding. Farther south, **Playa del Carmen**, once a tiny settlement, is now the fastest growing resort in the area. For many years Playa was simply a

The main town beach at Playa del Carmen

stepping-stone to Cozumel, only a 40-minute boat ride away – in fact the hotels along Cozumel's coastline can clearly be seen from the town jetty. But the town, sitting on a wonderful pale-sand beach with clear, bright azure water, has become an attraction in itself. It now boasts a variety of hotels and a pretty traffic-free street one block west of the strand, **Avenida 5** ('Fifth Avenue'), where the souvenir stores, cafés, and bars spill out into the street. As day turns to night, music from rock to reggae floats in the air. All this gives the town a lively atmosphere, but it still retains its appeal as a laid-back, cosmopolitan center with a distinctly European flair.

Xcaret

Beyond Playa the coastline is most dramatic; the limestone has been eroded into several coastal inlets, lagoons, and riverbeds. This stretch is excellent for snorkeling and has some exciting *cenotes* for diving and swimming; in addition, a number of these inlets have been protected as national parks or developed as pleasure playgrounds for tourists. Around 10km (6 miles) south of Playa del Carmen, **Xcaret** (pronounced shkaret; open daily 8.30am–9.30pm; admission fee) is the largest and the most organized resort, with a range of activities and facilities to enjoy. Xcaret, or 'little inlet,' is an award-winning example of a sustainable tourist development. Once the site of an ancient Maya port for departures to Cozumel, the sheltered lagoon was the perfect protection for Maya canoes. The waters of the nearby *cenote* were used for ritual purification before pilgrims made the short sea journey to the Temple of Ix-chel – the goddess of fertility and childbirth. The remains of several temples can be found in the park grounds.

When Xcaret opened in 1990, the *cenote* and its outlets to the sea were the focus of the park, and a swim along the Underground River or the Maya River is still one of the main attractions. But there is now much else besides, the park hav-

Maya warrior in the Ball Court at Xcaret

ing grown to include sheltered swimming, a beautiful beach, restaurants, tropical gardens, horseback-riding trails, a magnificent butterfly pavilion, a zoo, an aquarium, and a 'Swim with the Dolphins' program. The park is also contributing to a number of projects protecting endangered plants and animals, including the green turtle and several parrot species. As night falls, Xcaret holds a number of 'spectaculars' which are both entertaining and educational. Maya rituals are reenacted at the ancient sites, and there is a demonstration of the Maya Ball Game at the replica ball court. The Folkloric Show at the main amphitheater offers traditional music and dance from different regions in Mexico.

Puerto Aventuras and Xel-Ha

Puerto Aventuras is an interesting development, unlike any place else on the Maya Riviera. The rocky coastal inlets have been transformed into a magnificent marina, with mooring for yachts and motor launches and a walkway along the waterside. Two- and three-story pastel painted buildings line the marina, with restaurants at ground level. The whole area has the feel of the Italian or French Riviera rather than Caribbean Mexico. At the center of the resort, in the sheltered waters of the inner lagoon, there is a 'Swim with the Dolphins' program. Just beside the dolphin pools is the **Museo CEDAM** (Club de Exploración y Deporte Acuático de México), which is dedicated to a number of pioneers of underwater archaeology and exploration.

Just south of Puerto Aventuras is **Xel-Ha** (open daily 9am–6pm; admission fee), a network of mangrove, waterways, pools, and caves that was once a Maya site. The majority of the remains form an archaeological site on the landward side of the main highway; Xel-Ha Park sits on the seaward side. This managed park has more natural areas than Xcaret for snorkeling and exploring, but fewer organized activities, though there is a 'Swim with the Dolphins' program. At either side are public inlets; at **Akumal** you can snorkel just off the sand, or rent a boat to take you out to the reef.

South of Xel-Ha, and just to the west of Highway 307, is **Hidden Worlds Cenotes** (six scheduled snorkel tours and three diving tours daily), where anyone from novice snorkeler to fully qualified diver can explore the wonders of flooded caverns and *cenotes* lying just under the jungle floor, including the Dos Ojos Cenote and the aptly-named Bat Cave.

Snorkeling at Xel-Ha

Tulum

Tulum (open daily 8am–5pm; admission fee) is the most southerly destination of the tourist buses departing daily from Cancún. Buses and cars park some 700m (½ mile) from the entrance. There is an open-sided shuttle bus if you don't feel energetic enough for the walk.

The Maya ruins here are a magnet for visitors both for their architectural significance and their beautiful setting, being the only site fronting the open sea. Tulum was built late in Maya history, during the 12th century, and was still thriving in the 15th and 16th centuries when other Maya sites had been abandoned. This was a time of great upheaval, so the Maya built their temples close together and surrounded them with a strong defensive wall – the name Tulum actually means 'walled' or 'fenced.' The walls acted as a defense later in Maya history during the War of the Castes (1847), when several rebel Maya brought their families to hide out here.

There are no great structures on the scale of those at Chichén Itzá or Uxmal, but several sit on rocky outcrops overlooking the fine sandy beach and clear blue water below, making the place a photographer's delight. Chief among these is **El Castillo**, the main temple. Tulum was dedicated to the worship of the Descending God, who can be seen in carv-

Guide to the Maya Gods

The Maya worshiped a series of gods who they believed controlled their world. Each had its own sphere of responsibility that, when they worked together, provided full lives and good harvests. Here is a list of the most important:

Chaac: the god of rain, harvest, cenotes, lightning, tobacco, and the cardinal points.

Itzamná: the supreme god of creation, who gave the Maya corn, and written language.

Ix-chel: the goddess of women's fertility, medicine, childbirth, weaving, and the moon.

Kinich Ahau: the sun god.

Kukulcán (called *Quetzalcóatl* by the Toltecs): half god/half mortal who taught the Maya how to cultivate and use cocoa.

ings and stucco reliefs on El
Castillo and other buildings
at the site – though many
details have been lost to the
elements and the salt air. He
is depicted as a winged figure, head below and two feet
above. It is not clear what
this god's role was within
Maya worship; he may rep-
resent the setting sun, as
many temples at the site,
including El Castillo, face
west. A few steps northwest
of El Castillo is **Templo del
Dios Descendente** (The

Exploring Tulum

Temple of the Descending God), of note because it was delib-
erately built with walls and doors out of plumb.

Between the site entrance and El Castillo, the **Templo de
los Frescos** (Temple of the Frescoes or Paintings) has the
best-preserved reliefs at the site, and a rather worn stela
fronting the main facade. At each corner of the west-facing
wall it is possible to discern a somber mask with large eyes
and lips – possibly a depiction of Kukulcán. Above the
columned entrance are three niches, each with a relief of
the Descending God at the center. Red handprints decorate
the small upper room, and inside there are fine frescoes
dating to the 13th century, but it is not possible to enter the
temple to see them.

You can sunbathe on the beach at the site; some Mexican
families spend the day here, something the Maya would
never have been able to do when it was a religious center.
Only those who belonged to the upper and religious castes
were allowed into its inner sanctum.

Downtown Tulum has the feeling of a frontier town, though the road south toward the state capital, **Chetumal**, has recently been upgraded. Just east of downtown, along the coast, is a series of idyllic beaches, with a good choice of accommodations. From here it is possible to follow the Boca Paila Road to the south as far as Punta Allen, a good base from which to explore the **Sian Ka'an Biosphere Reserve** *(see page 69)*.

Cobá

Inland from Tulum is another Maya site worthy of note. **Cobá** (open daily 8am–5pm; admission fee) sits surrounded by jungle some 42km (26 miles) from Tulum on the banks of Lake Cobá. It is one of the largest Maya sites, said by archaeologists to be 100 sq km (39 sq miles) in area, and encompasses around 20,000 separate structures – though most have not been excavated. It is thought that at its peak (AD800–1000), it was one of the most important cities in the Maya world, with a network of roads reaching to many satellite settlements, some up to 100km (60 miles) away.

At Cobá it is possible to feel a little as Stephens and Catherwood did when they discovered the Maya sites in

Nohoch Mul pyramid, Cobá

their expeditions of 1841. Most of the pyramids and temples still lie under centuries of debris and vegetation, tantalizing visitors with intricate carvings peeking through roots and branches. Here you can imagine yourself to be exploring where no one except the abundant birds and butterflies has been for centuries. Cobá more than any other site

Stephens and Catherwood

When news of the Maya settlements of Guatemala and Belize first reached the outside world, two men – American diplomat John Lloyd Stephens and the English artist Frederick Catherwood – decided to travel to Yucatán to explore the region for more evidence. Their first expedition in 1841 almost ended in disaster, when Catherwood became ill with fever. However, the pair returned in 1843 and found the remains of many now-famous ancient sites, including Uxmal and Chichén Itzá.

Stephens wrote a fascinating account of the travels the pair undertook, illustrated by Catherwood's beautiful paintings. The works *Incidents of Travel in Central America, Chiapas, and Yucatán* and *Incidents of Travel in Yucatán* are still in print and would make a great accompaniment to your own explorations.

requires sensible footwear, hat, sunscreen, and bottled water, because the principal structures are spread so wide apart.

The main building at the site is the **Iglesia** or church, a huge pyramid nearly 30m (90ft) high. It sits among a number of structures known as the **Grupo Cobá**, which lie to the right of the main entrance. Its major staircase has been cleared, and the view from the top is spectacular, with the lakes and jungle stretching out to cover the land. At irregular intervals, vegetation-covered mounds indicate other pyramids yet to be freed. The only other large structure in view is the stone facade of **Nohoch Mul** (Big Hill) some 20 minutes' walk away. At 42m (138ft), Nohoch Mul is one of the tallest Maya pyramids ever discovered; there are 120 steps to its upper platform. Once there you will find images of the Descending God – the same image seen so often at Tulum. Between the Nohoch Mul group and Grupo Cobá is **Conjunto de las Pinturas** (Paintings Group) where you can see the Pyramid of the Painted Lintel, which, as the name suggests, still bears traces of its original coloring.

CANCÚN TO MÉRIDA

Traveling west out of the Cancún region transports you almost immediately into a different era. Traces of Spanish colonial life can be found across the landscape, but more than this, once out in the countryside the life of the agricultural worker very much resembles that lived by Maya in centuries past. Today they still produce numerous crops on their small farms *(milpas)*.

Two highways travel west: the four-lane toll highway carries traffic halfway across the Yucatán peninsula in around 3 hours; the local road travels through the countryside and many local settlements, giving an opportunity to view the daily life of the region. Both roads are numbered 180, but the local road is signposted '180 libre' (meaning free).

Valladolid's central plaza

Valladolid

The first major town on the 180 libre is **Valladolid**. Founded in 1543, it has the Yucatán's oldest church, **San Bernardino de Siena** (1552), now outshone by the imposing **Catedral de San Gervasio** in the main square. North of Valladolid on route 295 are the remains of the Maya city of **Ek Balam** (open daily 8am–5pm; admission fee). The scale of the buildings and their excellent restoration make this one of the most impressive Maya sites in the Yucatán. The main structures are grouped around two connecting spaces called the Central and Southern Plazas, with the Ball Court in between. At the north end of the site is the enormous main pyramid, or 'Acropolis', all of 160m (525ft) wide and 31m (100ft) high. On its restored flank is one of the most elaborate decorative friezes ever discovered in the Maya world, representing Itzamná, the God of Creation.

Continuing east, just before Chichén Itzá are the **Grutas de Balancanché** (Balancanché Caves; open daily 9am–5pm; self-guided tours in Spanish at 9am, noon, 2pm, and 4pm, English at 11am, 1pm, and 3pm), which were only rediscovered in 1959 after being abandoned by the Maya. The huge caverns with underground lakes were a place of offering, and evidence of incense burning can still be found.

Chichén Itzá

Three hours of traveling will bring you to the small town of **Pisté** and the remains of one of the most famous Maya sites. **Chichén Itzá** (open 8am–5pm; admission fee includes sound-and-light show in Spanish at 7pm and English at 8pm daily except Sun when admission is free) has fired the imagination of archaeologists and tourists alike. No matter how many other people happen to be there when you visit, you cannot help but be impressed by Chichén Itzá. It has been well excavated and the huge range of structures give a lasting impression of how life would have been lived by the Maya elite.

> Ik Kil *cenote*, just 2km (1 mile) before Chichén Itzá, is a great place for a cool swim. The *cenote* is open to the sky, with waterfalls and jungle creepers overhead. There is cabaña accommodation available, and a pleasant restaurant set in lush gardens.

The original Maya city at Chichén Itzá (Old Chichén) was built late in the empire's cycle, between 800 and 900 (the terminal classic period). Despite large amount of research, scientists are still not in agreement as to exactly how the city evolved, and what influences came to bear. What is certain is that Toltec influences, in the form of the god Quetzalcóatl (Kukulcán) and Chaac-Mool sculptures, can be found here, along with traditional Maya symbols. Another mystery yet to be solved is why the Toltec abandoned the city in 1200.

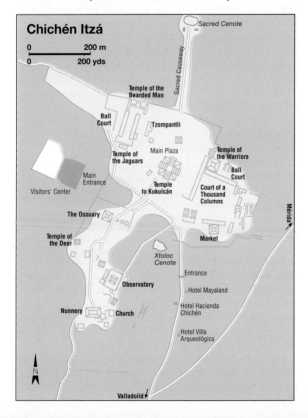

View of the Temple of Warriors from the Kukulcán Pyramid

Some time later, in the 13th century, the Itzá, a Maya tribe led by a ruler named Itzámna, moved north out of what is now the Campeche province to the tip of Yucatán and settled in the city. They gave the city the name Chichén Itzá, which means 'Mouth of the Well of the Itzás', and founded a capital at Mayapan, near the site of the modern city of Mérida. In the 15th century, following a bloody civil war, the Itzás abandoned Chichén Itzá and by the time the Spanish set foot on the peninsula it had already been reclaimed by the jungle.

Chichén Itzá occupies 6 sq km (4 sq miles). If you want to explore all corners of the site, a visit will occupy a full day. Excursions from Cancún are popular but can be tiring. It is far better to stay near the site (hotels adjacent to the site itself, in nearby Pisté and in Valladolid) and begin your visit early, because you can start when the day is cooler, and you will be able to see at least some of the site before the tour groups arrive. Those who stay overnight can also enjoy the sound-and-light show that takes place each evening. You can visit the site unaccompanied or hire a guide at the entrance, where there is a book and gift store, a restaurant, and a museum with finds from the site and a model of the city to help you to get your bearings.

The city has two distinct sectors. Old Chichén, in the south, is purely Puuc-Maya in style *(see page 70)*, having chambers with arched stone roofs. New Chichén has distinct Toltec influences; here stone columns supported roofs constructed with wooden beams. This allowed rooms in New Chichén to be much larger than in the older part of the site, but it also meant that as the wood rotted, the roofs of the chambers collapsed, leaving these structures less intact in the present day.

As you enter the site (in the new part of the city) the huge square edifice of **El Castillo**, also called the Pyramid of Kukulcán, comes into view on your right. The pyramid, 30m

El Castillo – a giant timepiece for the ancient Maya

(100ft) high and the main time-keeping mechanism of the city, was built very precisely in position, shape, and height in order to predict the planting and harvesting cycles. There are 364 steps in four staircases, which together with the final step up to the

> **Inside El Castillo are the foundations of an earlier structure, and a chamber containing the figure of a jaguar decorated with jade, along with a statue of Chaac, the Rain God.**

summit platform represent the 365 days of the year. There are 52 panels on each side, which echo the 52-year cycle of the Maya calendar, and terraces that parallel the main staircase, representing the 18-month solar cycle. The best time to see this super-sized timepiece in action is at the Spring Equinox (March 21) or Fall Equinox (September 21) in the afternoon, when the sun's rays fall down the northern stairway and hit the serpent head at the base. With the play of light and shadow, the serpent appears to wriggle down into the earth. For the Maya, this signified the refertilization of the land – and time to plant the corn. The light then leaves the snake head first and travels back up from the base; the Maya believed that the power of the sun was returning to the realm of the gods in the sky.

It is possible to climb one of the steep staircases to the upper platform, which has a number of small chambers. The view from the platform is spectacular; look down on other buildings on the site and also out to the distance, with the Yucatecan jungle stretching as far as the eye can see. Take care when you descend the staircase, as the treads are narrow.

To the left of the main entrance is the huge, open, main **Juego de Pelota** (ball court), one of the best preserved in Central America. Although one of nine on the site, it is definitely the most impressive, with walls 8m (26ft) high, 83m (272ft) long, and set 30m (98ft) apart. The walls are decorated with friezes showing players dressed in protective clothing and a rather bloodthirsty victor with the head of a losing player (though some archaeologists believe that the victor had the 'honor' of losing his life at the end of the match). This ball court has been well studied by archaeologists; ball courts can be found in most Mesoamerican settlements, but the true purpose of the games is still not fully understood.

There are temples at each end of the court, which add to the superb acoustics: it is possible to hear a voice speaking at one end clearly at the other, and the whole complex has a seven-repeat echo, a sacred number in Maya society. The temple attached to the eastern wall, the **Templo de los Jaguares** (Temple of the Jaguars), is named in honor of the jaguar figures carved on the upper panels of the temple and a statue of a jaguar in the lower chamber. The carving to its left is said to depict the Maya creation myth.

Next to the ball courts is **Tzompantli**, Temple of the Skulls, with long rows of skulls carved into its main platform. It is said that here the victims of sacrifice had their severed heads impaled on poles for the edification of the gods. Beside this is the **Plataforma de las Águilas** (Platform of the Eagles), with reliefs of eagles and jaguars clutching human hearts. Equidistant between El Castillo and the Temple of the Skulls, the **Plataforma de Venus** was dedicated to the worship of the planet Venus, a common deity among the Maya, and has motifs around its side which are thought to show the head of the planet emerging from a monster-serpent.

The Platform of Venus

From the Platform of Venus, a sacred causeway –

now little more than a dirt track – was once a paved highway to one of the most important religious sites in the city, the natural feature which may have given the city its name. The **Cenote Sagrado**, a limestone water-hole, 60m (90ft) in diameter and 21m (69ft) from rim to water level, was not a fresh water supply for the city; it had a much more chilling use. When archaeologists dredged the hole, hundreds of human bones, victims of the Maya ritual of appease-ment to the gods, were found. The skeletons of men, women, and children gave the *cenote* its other name, the Well of Sacrifice.

Chaac-Mool at the Temple of Warriors

To the east of the Platform of Venus is the striking **Templo de los Guerreros** (Temple of the Warriors). Named for the reliefs depicting thousands of Maya warriors, the temple also has numerous columns, putting one in mind of a classi-cal Greek edifice. On a platform above the columns is a carved figure of Chaac-Mool in reclining position, its belly hollowed into a bowl to receive offerings – some experts think these included human hearts fresh from the body.

Reached through a colonnaded walkway abutting the Temple of the Warriors is what modern archaeologists have named the **Mercado** or Market, with the remains of steam baths and a number of ball courts. Just south of the market

El Caracol – the Observatory

are the tracks of the modern road (now diverted) that once cut through the site. Beyond this are remains to the south and west – Old Chichén. Directly ahead is the **Tumba del Gran Sacerdote** (Tomb of the High Priest) built atop a limestone cave where human sacrifices were carried out. Several small temples can be found here. **Casa de los Metates** (the House of the Grinding Stones) is named after the corn-grinding stones of the Maya, which are used in villages in the region in the present day. Several were found here when archaeologists investigated the building. **Chichan-chob** (Little Holes, also called Red House) is an older-style building in the Puuc style. It has small holes in the roof and masks of Chaac-Mool on the upper walls.

Beyond a small ball court, you will see the imposing building of the observatory, **El Caracol**. An important place for the inhabitants of the city, observations taken here would predict the exact times of the equinoxes and important celestial events. El Caracol means 'the snail' in Spanish; it was given its name by explorer John Lloyd Stephens because he thought that the spiral staircase on the inside of the dome mimicked the chamber of a snail shell.

Edificio de las Monjas (Edifice of the Nuns), lying farthest south, is perhaps the most Puuc in style *(see page 70)* of all the buildings here. It stands on the site of much older buildings that can be seen in the interior. Nearby is a building called, surprisingly, **La Iglesia** (The Church). It isn't a place of Christian worship – in fact it is one of the oldest buildings on the site, and pays homage to the *bacah*, a group of gods thought to have held up the sky. Images of snail and tortoise can be seen here, among others. The walls of **Akab Dzib**, the Temple of Obscure Writing, to the east of the Church, are filled with Maya glyphs, the written language of the people that has been the focus of much attention and research in the last 30 years.

Other buildings of Old Chichén lie in the scrubland to the south of these structures, but exploration is more difficult and you may benefit from having a guide.

Izamal

Farther west is the small town of **Izamal**. The settlement is known as 'the city of three cultures' because, perhaps more than anywhere in the region, you can find Maya, colonial, and modern influences together in the city streets. At the heart of the city is the **Monastery of San Antonio de Padua**,

Monastery of San Antonio de Padua, Izamal

Maya woman in Izamal

home to the Franciscan order and founded by Archbishop de Landa in the 16th century. Today there are 10 monks continuing the tradition, though only their inner sanctum is out of bounds, leaving you free to explore the small courtyards and chapels. In 1993, Pope John Paul II visited the monastery, conducting a Mass here. A small museum has photographs of his visit, along with a papal throne built especially for the occasion.

The monastery and buildings on the surrounding streets – rows of old colonial houses – have been painted a bright yellow, one of the traditional colors used by the Spanish settlers. You can take a *calesa* ride through the streets and visit the remains of Maya structures, including **Kinich Kakmo** ('the face of the maker of the sun'). With its base covering an entire block almost 200m (219 yds) square, and topped by a smaller pyramid, this is in fact the largest known structure of the entire Maya world. There are superb views of Izamal and its surroundings from the top.

Mérida

The largest city on the Yucatán peninsula and capital of Yucatán state, La Blanca **Mérida** was founded in the 1640s, at the very start of the Spanish occupation, on the site of a large Maya city, T'Ho. Mérida became the focus of influence for the Montejo family, who exerted their force over the surrounding countryside. Since that time, it has seen the ebb

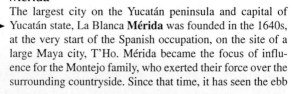

and flow of economic prosperity and political power, yet its architecture and lifestyle – a total contrast to modern Cancún – make it a fascinating place to visit. Mérida is a vibrant, bustling city with a tangible energy. It also has interesting attractions that can fill a few days of your itinerary.

The heart of the city is **Plaza Grande** (also known by a variety of names such as Plaza des Armas, Plaza Principal, Plaza de la Independencia, and Plaza de la Revolucion). Its tree-lined center has shaded seats where everyone comes to meet and talk; shoe-shine boys work throughout the day, while ice-cream sellers stand on street corners with their small barrows. Look out for the *confidenciales,* or love seats, where courting couples could sit next to each other without compromising the woman's reputation. In the center of the square is a flagpole supporting a Mexican flag, which is raised and lowered at the start and end of each day (6am and 6pm) in an elaborate ceremony undertaken by the local police band. Numerous historic buildings, dating back to the very earliest days of Spanish rule, line the square and its surrounding grid of streets. Construction of many of these buildings used stones from the Maya city of T'Ho, so, alas, nothing remains of this site.

Mérida's cathedral

Perhaps the most important building is **Palacio de Montejo**, on the south side of the square. It was built as a family home for the Montejo dynasty and was completed in 1549. The facade – now the only original element of the house – is decorated with a number of ornate carvings, including two large conquistadors seen treading on the heads of Maya Indians. Perhaps this decoration was added to reaffirm Montejo power in the region. The style of the house is pure Spanish-colonial, with an inner courtyard garden lined by rooms with high ceilings and huge wooden doors. The house was in the Montejo family until the 1970s but then passed into the hands of a bank, which now operates a regional office, ATM, and currency exchange in the interior. Visitors can wander into the courtyard, but many of the architectural treasures are off-limits.

On the west of the square is the **Palacio Municipal** (City Hall). Inside you can see the wood-lined Sala de

The courtyard of the Governor's Palace

Cabildos, where the board of the city still holds its regular meetings. The northern side of the square is taken up by the **Palacio del Gobierno** (Governor's Palace; open daily 8am–10pm; free), now merely an administrative building, but once the Governor's residence. There is a tourist information office just inside the entrance, and in the inner courtyard hang many large canvases by artist Fernando Castro Pancheco illustrating important incidents and individuals in Yucatán's history. On the second floor, the Salon de Historia, a long gallery once used for social soirées, has more paintings that complete the collection.

The eastern side of the square is dominated by the **Catedral** (1561), one of the oldest in the Americas. Inside you will find the large crucifix christened **Cristo de las Ampollas** (Christ of the Blisters), which has been on display here since 1645. It was carved in the 1500s out of wood from a miraculous tree, so called because it had caught fire but did not burn. Later the finished crucifix survived another disastrous fire, though its surface was blistered. Just behind the Catedral on Calle 61 is the **Museo de la Ciudad** (open Tues–Fri 10am–2pm and 4–8pm, Sat–Sun 10am–2pm; free), which displays drawings, maps, plans, and photographs relating to the planning and growth of Mérida.

Next to the Catedral is the **Museo Macay** (Museum of Contemporary Art; open Wed–Sun 10am–5pm; admission fee), which occupies a colonial building at the site of the archbishop's palace, now destroyed. The gallery exhibits some interesting works of modern art, with permanent exhibitions of Yucatecan and other Mexican artists, and a comprehensive program of temporary exhibitions.

The Plaza Major sits in a square between calles 60 and 62 and calles 61 and 63 (even street numbers run east–west, odd street numbers run north–south); the surrounding streets boast numerous colonial gems that can only be appreciated

Plaza de la Maternidad, along Calle 60

by strolling around the town. For those with little time to spare, **Calle 60** has the most concentrated collection.

One block north of Plaza Mayor along Calle 60, you will pass **Parque Hidalgo**, dominated by the Jesuit-built church, La Tercera Orden. Built in 1618, this church contains a painting that depicts the meeting in 1546 of Montejo and Tutul Xiú, the Maya ruler, who became a convert to Christianity, thus inducing most other local chiefs to follow his lead.

Beyond the church is another small square, **Plaza de la Maternidad**, which has a sculpture of *Mother and Child*, a copy of the Renoir piece in Paris. The **Teatro Peón Contreras** occupies the northern corner of the square, with a Parisian-style café on its first floor and a regular schedule of performances. The theater is a splendid example of late 19th- to early 20th-century architecture, with a sweeping marble staircase leading to a colonnaded upper balcony. Across the street is the **Universidad de Yucatán**. One block farther north is

Parque Santa Lucía, with the array of busts in its 'Poet's Corner' commemorating the Yucatán's cultural and artistic greats, including Cirilo Baquiero, father of Yucatecan song.

If you are walking, make a right at Calle 47 past Parque Santa Anna, then left at the traffic signal. This is **Paseo Montejo**, one of the finest streets in the city, known by citizens of Mérida as 'the Champs-Elysèes of Yucatán.' This tree-lined avenue was *the* place to live during the 19th century, and all the best families and rich henequen producers vied for the best plots along its length. The houses they built still have an elegance and stature, though many have been lost to modern development.

The most impressive of the remaining period buildings is Palacio Canton, which now houses the **Museo Regional de Antropología e Historia** (Regional Anthropological and History Museum; open Tues–Sat 8am–8pm, Sun 8am–2pm; admission fee). The beautiful plasterwork detail and marble floors of the palace are only surpassed by the wealth of Maya artifacts on display. The displays illustrate the most recent theories on Maya society including trade patterns and social customs. On the second floor of the museum, exhibitions relate the methods used to excavate various sites around Yucatán. The museum is an excellent starting point for your tour of the Maya sites.

North from the museum, at a major intersection on the Paseo, is the **Monumento a la Patria** (Monument to the Fatherland, or National Monument). This huge limestone monument depicting Maya, Spanish, and Mexican themes was begun in 1944 and completed in 1956.

Mérida and culture go hand in hand. The city holds artistic and folkloric performances on every night of the week and an 'all-day' event in the heart of the city on Sundays. See the 'What to Do' section *(page 92)* for more details.

Locals cool off in the *cenote* at the temple ruins of Dzibilchaltún

Dzibilchaltún

Although the Maya city of T'Ho has been completely swallowed by colonial Mérida, a 10-minute taxi ride north of the city is **Dzibilchaltún** (open daily 8am–5pm; admission fee) a city that thrived from 3000BC on a marine economy – the coast being only 32km (20 miles) away. Archaeologists believe that at its peak in the late classic period (AD600–800) the population reached 20,000, and that the function of the city changed over time from ceremonial to urban.

El Templo de las Siete Muñecas (called the Doll's House, in English) is the most interesting structure at the site; it is the only Maya building with windows to be found so far, though these are not thought simply to have provided light for the room. The openings together with the doors frame the five segments of the sky marked by the solstices, the equinoxes, and the zenith. When archaeologists were excavating the building they found seven small clay dolls, each with a bodily deformity. No one is sure whether these were simply a child's toys or if they had a religious significance, but they gave the structure its name. The dolls are on display at the museum found just beyond the site entrance.

To the north of Dzibilchaltún, on the coast at the end of Highway 261, lies **Progreso**, the closest beach town to Mérida and a popular vacation spot for locals.

Eco-attractions in the Northern Yucatán

There has been a great deal of development in the northern Yucatán during the last 30 years. But with acres of forest, coastline, and lagoons, along with thousands of *cenotes* and hundreds of caves, it is no surprise that the area has a number of national parks and protected sites offering the opportunity to explore pristine natural environments.

North of Isla Mujeres is the tiny **Isla Contoy**, which is a bird sanctuary and wildlife preserve with large populations of gulls and frigate birds. You can reach it by boat from Isla Mujeres.

Río Lagartos on the coast north of Valladolid is a large lagoon and mangrove swamp, the breeding-ground for a huge flock of Caribbean flamingos. It also has small populations of crocodile, deer, boar, and jaguar.

Celestún to the west of Mérida has the vast **Flamingo Mexicano de Celestún**, a summer feeding ground for the flamingos and their chicks, along with myriad other sea birds.

South of Tulum is the huge **Sian Ka'an Biosphere Reserve**, at 6,000 sq km (2,300 sq miles), the largest in the region. Much of this area, with mixed environments of mangrove, savanna, *cenote* and coral reef, has no human population, making it a suitable environment for the endangered jaguar as well as monkeys, deer, wild pig, birds, and mangrove-dwelling creatures. Day excursions can be organized from Cancún, but you must be accompanied by a guide. Tel: 998/884 9583 for further details.

THE PUUC ROUTE

The region to the south of Mérida is known as the **Puuc** (pronounced 'pook'). It has the highest ground in Yucatán, the 'Sierrita Puuc' – a ridge of limestone hills 50m (150ft) in height, and thought to be the edge of a giant crater formed when a meteorite fell to earth millions of years ago. Today the land is home to communities of Maya farmers, but the jungle has relinquished a number of fine ancient sites to explore. These sites are called Puuc sites, and this name has also been taken to describe the characteristics of the architecture and design of the buildings here. The Puuc style is characterized by ornate decoration, with latticework carving on the lower facades and masks and carvings on the upper levels.

The Maya settlements of the region were very rich. The fertile land enabled several crops a year to be harvested, and the surpluses thus produced allowed the community to support artisans such as stonemasons and to trade with other communities for goods and raw materials not naturally available locally.

On the route south from Mérida you'll travel through countryside once filled with haciendas (old colonial farms).

Mask detail at Kabáh

When the henequen boom was at its height, the number of haciendas grew dramatically, but when the system was dismantled in 1937 most fell into decline. The hacienda consisted of a main house surrounded by its land, a factory, and a village for the hacienda workers. This would include a school and a company store where workers were forced to buy their supplies. Many of the modern villages of this region have their roots in the hacienda system. As you pass through them you may see an old chimney breaking above the tree line, a sure sign that the village was once part of a hacienda.

Hacienda Yaxcopoil

Head out of Mérida on Highway 180 as if going to Campeche, but at Uman go south along the 261. At km 33, you'll pass the village of Yaxcopoil, dominated on the right-hand side of the road by the enormous **Hacienda Yaxcopoil** (open Mon–Sat 8am–6pm, Sun 9am–1pm; admission fee), now the Yucatán's principal hacienda museum.

Hacienda Yaxcopoil

The buildings are well preserved, but not overly restored – it's as if time has stood still. The main building, entered through an archway, consists of two parallel ranges. In the left-hand range, with its high ceilings, is the office, the living room, reception room, bedrooms, bathroom, and chapel, all with original period furnishings. The other range houses the kitchen and dining room, as well as the Maya Room, where pieces of pottery and other finds from the small ruins scattered around the estate are on display. It's also possible to visit the factory, complete with machinery. Opposite the main building is a Maya village, its inhabitants descendants of the Maya who once worked on the huge estate.

Uxmal

Uxmal (open daily 8am–5pm; admission fee including sound-and-light show in Spanish at 7pm and English at 8pm daily except Sun when admission is free) is considered the jewel of Maya sites in Yucatán, its buildings richly decorated with elaborate carvings. At its peak between AD600–900 it is said to have had a population of around 25,000 – remarkable when you consider that it had no water supply and had to collect and store its needs artificially.

One of the highlights of the site presents itself immediately as you enter. The magnificent **Pirámide del Advino** (Pyramid of the Magician, also called the Pyramid of the Dwarf) sits atop five older structures. This pyramid is unique for a number of reasons. It has rounded sides, giving it a softened shape. It's steep (even more precipitous than the normal elevations in the area), and the design of the doorway at the top, which is a huge representation of Chaac, is found at no other site. The facade of the upper levels is extremely ornate and the main staircase has a parallel row of large Chaac masks. The pyramid has recently been restored, and the steep climb to the top is well worth it for the magnificent views of the site and surrounding jungle.

The Speedy Life of the Dwarf

Mayan legend has it that the dwarf who built the Temple of the Dwarf at Uxmal hatched from an egg and grew to adulthood during his first day of life. He spent his first night constructing the temple, which was complete by sunrise the next day.

Modern archaeological research is uncovering evidence that the dwarf of mythology may have actually been a real person – statues show a ruler who was short even by Maya standards – who could have contributed greatly to the building of this important city.

**The Governor's Palace at Uxmal, with the
Pyramid of the Magician in the background**

Next to the pyramid is the **Cuadrángulo de las Monjas**
(Nunnery Quadrangle), given its name in the 16th century
because it resembled a Spanish monastery or nunnery. Its
size – over 70 rooms – has caused archaeologists to postu-
late that it may have been a military academy, which expanded regularly throughout its history. The western
building has the most richly carved facade. There are also
numerous depictions of Maya homes or *na*, which can still
be found all across the countryside of Yucatán. The eastern
building has a statue of a dwarf dressed in a turtle shell
placed in a position normally associated with the rulers of
Maya cities. A serpent is entwined all along the upper facade
around the statue. From its upper levels the many buildings
at the site come clearly into view. The quadrangle is the setting for the **Uxmal Sound-and-Light Show**, which takes
place every evening except Sunday.

South of the quadrangle, beyond a small ball court, the land rises to a higher level. Here another group of buildings forms the main center of focus at the site. The **Casa de las Tortugas** (Turtle House), so called because of numerous turtle motifs adorning it, is found immediately on the right. Beside, and totally dwarfing it, lies the **Palacio del Gobernador**

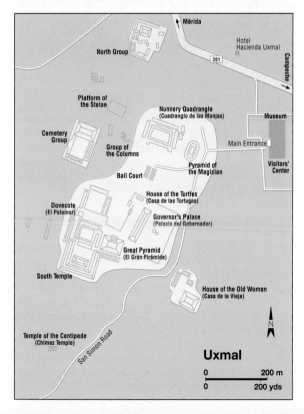

(Governor's Palace) with an imposing 100-m (320-ft) long facade. The building was erected in the 11th century for the ruler of the city, Halach Huinic ('the true man'), and consists of a central building flanked by two smaller wings. The frieze of Chaac masks is one of the most ornate and complex in the known Maya world.

Archway into the Nunnery Quadrangle

Behind the palace is the **Great Pyramid**; it is less ornate than the palace, and only the front facade has been restored. Beyond this area, there are several other groups of buildings, many of which have yet to be excavated, including the Dovecote Group (which includes the **Casa de las Palomas**, the House of Doves) and the **Grupo del Cementario** (Cemetery Group). Beyond these are several even more remote sites that can be visited, but you would benefit from the services of a guide to find them.

Other Puuc Sites

Uxmal was a very rich city at the height of its powers and protector of many smaller settlements, which paid tribute to it both in food and money. A string of these sites now forms what is called the Puuc Route, and they can all be visited in one day. Though small, each one has something different to reveal.

First in the tour is **Kabáh**, only 27km (17 miles) south of Uxmal. The major structure at the site is the **Codz-Pop** or Palace of the Masks, constructed in Chenes style – characterized by masks covering the whole facade of the structure from ground to roof. There are said to have been over 250 Chaac representations – a most impressive sight unique in the Maya world. Codz-Pop means 'rolled-up sleeping mat,' referring to the curled-up nose on the masks. Cross the main road dividing the site to find a restored archway, which once marked the end of a *sacbé* (sacred Maya road) from Uxmal.

Eight kilometers (5 miles) south of Kabah is **Sayil**, famed for its major building, called **El Palacio** (the Palace) by the Spanish. With over 100 rooms, it would be important for its size alone, but the ornate decoration makes it even more impressive, with representations of the Descending God found so prominently at Tulum.

Nearby **Xlapak** has only one major structure – a palace – but **Labná**, the final Puuc site on the tour, has a number of structures to explore. **El Palacio** here is decorated with alli-

The facade of the Palace at Sayil

gators whose open jaws each have a human head emerging from them. This symbol, called Pop, is thought to be indicative of power and is only found at this site. A *sacbé* links the palace to other parts of the site. The tallest structure is the **Mirador**, a pyramid temple over 20m (65ft) high. Next to the Mirador is the most famous sight in Labná, also much changed since its discovery. **El Arco** (the Arch), is late Puuc style

The Loltún Caves

and was thought to have been the entrance to the courtyard of a family residence. Though the arch remains, two ornate walls at either side of it collapsed during the 20th century.

Before leaving the Puuc area, visit the **Loltún Caves** (tours daily at 9.30am, 11am, 12.30pm, 2pm, 3pm, and 4pm; admission fee). On the guided tour through these impressive caverns you can see evidence of where the Maya rebels fortified the entrances during the War of the Castes in the 1840s.

The Convent Route

From the Loltún Caves, it's an easy detour north to **Maní**, where the Church of San Miguel Arcángel was the site of Bishop Diego de Landa's ritual burning of the Maya manuscripts in 1562. Mani is just one settlement along the so-called Convent Route, which you can follow by taking Highway 18 for the return to Mérida. There are a number of Franciscan-built monasteries and churches to visit, as well as the important ancient city of **Mayapan**.

WHAT TO DO

SHOPPING

Traveling around the Yucatán peninsula will present you with a wealth of shopping opportunities – many are only a short stroll away from the beaches. Cancún has a number of modern, air-conditioned shopping malls with internationally recognized brand names, where you can shop in comfort from morning to night, though of course prices are higher here than inland. For strolling and browsing in the Mexican sunshine or the cooler air of the evening, there are shopping streets in San Miguel de Cozumel, Isla Mujeres, and on Avenida 5 in Playa del Carmen. These streets have stores selling locally produced crafts, jewelry, and imported goods, and pretty boutiques.

Visit the Hi Kuic craft market in downtown Cancún, and better still the Mercado Municipal in Mérida, to experience the genuine, colorful atmosphere of a Mexican market. Examples of every locally produced craft can be found in abundance here, and you'll shop less expensively than in the resorts, especially if you practice your bartering skills beforehand.

Don't let the range of goods blind you to low quality or fakes. Always examine the item you want very carefully and shop around to get a feel of the prices before you buy. Most stores in the main tourist areas will stay open until 9 or 10pm. Prices will often be quoted, and you will be able to pay, in US dollars.

As you shop, be aware that certain items are made from protected species. It is illegal to sell tortoiseshell and black coral products, both of which are also illegal to import into Australia, the EU, and the US.

What to Buy

Handicrafts. The Maya people have always made everything they needed, and their handicrafts, though often practical, make beautiful souvenirs. Basketware made from sisal and other plants found in the area is typically used to carry a range of goods; woven mats can also be found. Hammocks come in a bewildering range of quality, colors, and sizes; you'll have your choice of a *sencillo* (single) or one to share with friends, such as a *doble* (double) or *matrimonial* (family-sized).

Weaving has also been a very important skill for the Maya. The fabric produced on personal looms in traditional patterns and colors is used in a variety of different products. *Sarapes*, cotton or wool blankets, and rugs are popular, but you will also find the material made into jackets and hats.

Baskets are often made by hand by women in colorful *huipiles*

Maya themes. The Maya have a special place in the imagination and their traditional motifs and copies of their ceremonial artifacts make popular souvenirs. Carvings of the gods, Chaac Mool in particular, along with revered creatures such as the jaguar or the feathered serpent, are produced in stone, onyx, silver, wood, and papier-mâché, in sizes from a lucky talisman for your purse to a sculpture for your garden.

Ceremonial masks are also very beautiful and can be found in a range of qualities and sizes. Made from papier-mâché that is smoothed and brightly painted, they make beautiful wall decorations.

Pottery and glass. Terracotta pots have been the basic cooking utensil for generations of Maya families. You'll find these in various sizes and with different decoration. Blown glassware is also exquisite; bowls, jugs, vases, and glasses can be bought throughout the region.

Replica of a Maya figurine from the island of Jaína

Silver. Mexico is one of the largest producers of silver in the world. There is an amazing range of jewelry available, such as chains, earrings, and finger and toe rings, and prices are very competitive. Larger pieces such as tea-sets and goblets can be found in the bigger stores, as can silver pill-boxes, purses, or small 'sombreros.' Always make sure that your purchase bears a stamp of the word Mexico and of the numbers 925 (the standard quality of silver found here) or 960 (purer but slightly softer). This ensures that you are buying genuine silver.

Tequila and other alcohol. Tequila is the national drink of Mexico, made from the distilled juice of the agave plant (100% agave tequila is the best quality), and it can be bought under numerous trade names. It is produced only in a very small region of Mexico, around the town of Tequila near Guadalajara, and is in reality a refined version of the agave drink Mezcal. You can also take home a bottle of the Yucatecan liquor Xtebentun, with its flavor of anise, honey, and flowers.

Clothing. You are sure to find something that fits your personal taste in summer attire in the Yucatán. Designer labels from the US and Europe are abundant in the tourist-zone malls in Cancún. Smaller stores throughout the region are filled with attractive beachwear, T-shirts, hats, footwear, and cool, comfortable cotton dresses, skirts, and sarongs that are ideal for the warm climate here.

Locally produced cottons and woven garments are sold in craft markets and stores. The colorful patterns have been handed down through the generations. In the countryside, the Maya women still wear the traditional *huipile*, a loose cotton slip with embroidered detail; the everyday version has stitching around the neckline and hem, the ceremonial version several layers of embroidery and lace. In Mérida, the men wear the *guayabera*, a short-sleeved linen or cotton shirt with finely pleated front detail, worn untucked. These tend to be much cooler than fitted shirts. *Huaraches* are hand-fashioned leather sandals with sisal thongs. You can top off your whole traditional ensemble with a hat: local people wear good quality panama hats (many imported from Guatemala). You can also buy sombreros, though these are actually traditional in regions of Mexico other than Yucatán.

Duty-Free Shopping

Cozumel is a major cruise destination and as such offers goods like fragrances and gemstones at duty-free prices. You can buy loose stones or finished pieces at a number of large, air-conditioned stores on Avenida Melgar, with prices said to be as much as 40 percent lower than US retail. If you intend to make a major purchase of this type while visiting the region, it would be wise to research the prices and quality of goods at home before you travel, so that you can be sure you are getting a good deal.

Snorkelers in the Underground River at Xcaret

SPORTS

Diving

Cancún, Cozumel, and the Maya Riviera offer some of the most pristine waters for diving and a wealth of natural reefs and artificial dive sites to explore. They are still considered some of the best sites in the world, despite the explosion in the number of divers over recent years. The lack of soil and rivers on the Yucatecan mainland mean that there is no silt in the sea to reduce underwater visibility, and there is little heavy industry in the area to pollute the ocean, leaving the marine life relatively healthy.

The island of Cozumel is still regarded as the jewel among diving areas. There are 30km (20 miles) of reef at many different depths off the western coast. Divers have a chance to see turtles, sharks, and barracuda in their natural environment; the warm waters make for exciting and comfortable diving throughout the year. In addition, there are opportunities for both certified divers and those who would like to earn their certification.

Cancún is a great beginner's resort; it has many shallow dive sites suitable for the novice. Experts can be well rewarded too – just a short distance from your hotel are challenging dive sites and some of the richest marine life anywhere on earth. Remember to bring your dive certificate, as you will only be allowed to rent equipment and dive if you can prove your competence.

Choice Dive Sites

Cozumel

Cantarell. Soft coral and sponges, nurse sharks, rays, turtles; 11–30m (35–90ft).

Palancar Reef. Off the west coast; three areas with large coral formations at 8m (25ft), relatively shallow and good for novice divers. Palancar Caves have passages through coral formations; grouper and turtles; starting at about 10m (35ft).

San Francisco Reef. Dive wall in relatively shallow water; lots of marine life.

Santa Rosa Reef. Deep with strong current; challenging reef dive.

Chankanaab Shallows. Near the National Park, good for novice divers; marine life, abundant lobster and other crustaceans; 10–16m (30–50ft).

Chankanaab Reef. Sea turtles, rays, amberjack, huge grouper; reefs starting at 16–30m (50–90ft) falling off to a deep abyss.

Isla Mujeres

Manchones Reef. Just off the southeastern tip of the island, where the water is 5 to 11m (15-35ft) deep.

Banderas Reef. Stunningly beautiful colors and an abundance of marine life can be observed here at just 12m (40ft).

If you want to learn to dive in Cancún and Cozumel, there is an excellent network of dive centers offering training to professional levels. All centers are affiliated with one of the major certifying bodies, NAUI (National Association of Underwater Instructors) or PADI (Professional Association of Diving Instructors), the latter being the most common. The basic qualification, the Open Water certificate, takes five days to complete. Upon completion you can dive with an instructor to a depth of 18m (60ft), which opens to you many sites in the region. Diving centers also offer an introductory session known as the 'Discover Scuba Program,' which includes a morning or afternoon of theory and swimming-pool work to give you the chance to practice the basic techniques. Many large hotels offer this lesson as a facility for their guests.

The following are reputable local dive centers: **Diving Adventures**, Calle 5 Sur #22, Cozumel, tel: 987/872-3009, <www.divingadventures.net>; **Scuba Cancún**, km 5 Paseo Kukulcán, lagoon side, Cancún, tel: 998/849-7508, <www.scubacancun.com.mx>; **Sea Friends**, Avenida Hidalgo s/n, Playa Norte, Isla Mujeres, tel: 998/842-5348.

Snorkeling

Well over half of all visitors to the region will snorkel while on vacation. The superb clarity and warmth of the water, the abundant sea life even in the shallows, and the proximity of all of this to the resorts are what make snorkeling here appealing. You can snorkel at just about every beach on the west coast of Cozumel, on Isla Mujeres, and along the Riviera Maya. The many national parks offer more natural environments, though the sea may still be crowded with fellow snorkelers during the high season. Garrafón/Punta Sur Park on Isla Mujeres and Chankanaab National Park on Cozumel both rent snorkeling equipment.

Cavern Diving at Hidden Worlds

The inlets along the Riviera Maya are a perfect environment for small, brightly colored tropical fish. Xcaret is probably the most famous site, but you can enjoy snorkeling at Xel-Ha and Trés Rios as well.

Not yet qualified to dive? Both SNUBA and BOB are half-and-half water experiences. With both you are underwater, but with a constant supply of air from tubes at the surface. BOB, the Breathing Observation Bubble, is a kind of underwater scooter with oxygen helmet. Contact **Hotel Cancún Marina Club**, km 5.5 (tel: 998/883-4440), for details. With SNUBA you wear a helmet, but you walk on the ocean floor. Contact AquaWorld in Cancún for further details.

Cavern Diving/Snorkeling

The freshwater *cenotes* and caverns of the peninsula offer another fascinating dimension to diving, and indeed snorkeling. A number of dive companies offer excursions, or you can go direct to Hidden Worlds Cenotes *(see page 47)*, which runs diving and snorkeling tours into the world's largest system of underwater caverns, just north of Tulum. Even novice snorkelers can admire the cavernous, crystal-clear depths here; for divers an open water certificate is sufficient. **Hidden Worlds**, tel: 984/877-8535; <www.hiddenworlds.com.mx>.

Other Activities

Swim with the Dolphins. These programs exist at various locations around the region, so you will have the opportunity no matter which of the big resorts you choose. Some venues have a range of different programs, from simply free-swimming with dolphins, to performing exercises with them, to helping a trainer for a day. Dolphin Discovery operates programs at Isla Mujeres, Cozumel, and Puerto Aventuras; <www.dolphindiscovery.com>. Other programs can be found at Xel-Ha and Xcaret.

Viewing marine life without getting wet. If getting into the water isn't for you, then take a glass-bottom boat ride; trips navigate the mangrove swamps or venture out to the ocean reefs. It is also possible to travel under the surface of the water in a submersible craft. *Nautibus, Sub See Explorer*, and *Atlantis XII* all submerge to 50m (150ft) to explore the reef ecosystem. *Nautibus* has four sailings a day: El Embarcadero, km 4 Cancún Hotel Zone, tel: 998/883-

With the dolphins at Chankanaab State Park

3732. **AquaWorld** boasts various craft as well – they can be found at Kukulcán Boulevard, km 15.2 Hotel Zone, tel: 998/848-8326; <www.aquaworld.com.mx>. Atlantis Submarine: Chankanaab km 4, Casa del Mar Hotel, Cozumel, tel: 987/872-5671 or (888) REAL-SUB (toll-free in the US); <www.goatlantis.com>.

Beach and Swimming Notes

With over 14km (9 miles) of unbroken white sand, it is not surprising that most people list the beach as the main reason for visiting Cancún; in fact nine named beaches cover the whole 27-km (17-mile) strand. The whole Riviera Maya also has some wonderful sandy beaches, as do the islands of Cozumel and Isla Mujeres. The following list describes some of the best.

Playa Tortuga, Cancún. Sheltered from the Caribbean waves by Isla Mujeres; great for snorkeling and swimming.

Playa Chaac Mool, Cancún. Close to all of the Hotel Zone's activities, bars, and shopping.

Playa Norte, Isla Mujeres. At the northern tip of the island, with beautiful sand and shady palms.

San Francisco Beach and Playa Palancar, Cozumel. Both fine-sand beaches with good facilities and crystal-clear turquoise water.

Playa del Carmen. Eclectic and European; topless and nude bathing allowed to the north of Coco Beach.

Swimmers should beware of dangerous currents and undertows, particularly along the exposed stretches of coast. The local authorities have a code system, consisting of colored flags hung at public beaches and at major hotels, to inform visitors about the condition of the sea.

White flag: Perfect or excellent conditions.

Green flag: Normal conditions; safe for swimming.

Yellow flag: Use caution; situation changing or conditions uncertain.

Red or black flag: Conditions unsafe for swimming.

Watersports. Most of the major resorts will have water 'toys' for rent; you can jet-ski or water-bike in the Caribbean or along the Mangrove swamps in the lagoon at Cancún. Note: Do obey the speed limits, in place to protect the delicate environment that is damaged by waves from speeding boats and jet-skis. And what better way to view the beautiful landscape, particu-

Beach volleyball is a popular pursuit

larly the long beach and lagoon at Cancún, than from a parasail some 33m (100ft) up in the air? You'll be able to fully appreciate the color of the sand and the ocean from on high.

Sport fishing. The warm waters of the Caribbean are teeming with fish, and sport fishing is becoming increasingly popular. Bonito, amberjack, barracuda, and shark can be caught in these waters all year; huge sailfish, tuna, and several species of marlin are most common between March and June; and in the winter months shoals of grouper and jewfish abound. Large, powerful boats can be organized at just about every resort along the coast – they are particularly plentiful in Cozumel and Playa del Carmen. The local guides are especially experienced and helpful. You can also go fly-fishing in the Nichupté Lagoon and the lagoons of the Sian Ka'an Biosphere Reserve, where catching four different types of fish (bonefish, permit, snook, and tarpon) constitutes a so-called Grand Slam. Operators practice catch and release, and special hooks ensure that the fish are not harmed.

Golf. Cancún has a growing number of golf courses, and the climate of the area is ideal for a round or two. Pok-Ta-Pok was the first course, and some still say the best. However, since it opened, several large hotels have built courses as part of their guest facilities: The Meliá Cancún, km 15; The Hilton Cancún Beach and Golf Resort, km 17; and The Westin Regina, km 19.5. There are several courses along the Maya Riviera, principally at Puerto Aventuras, and Playacar courses are located in Playa del Carmen.

Horseback riding. The Spanish introduced horses to the region, and they were perfect for transport through the 'low jungle.' Today you can explore the area on horseback, enjoying organized and guided trails at many parks, such as Xcaret and Trés Rios. All across the region you will see ranches advertising their services – often you will see a horse tied in the shade at the ranch entrance to indicate that riding is offered.

Hitting the trail

Birdwatching. Protected lagoons and mangroves at Río Lagartos and Celestún provide a haven for a rich variety of birdlife. The fragile ecosystem of the lagoons, with their shallow hypersaline waters, provides the perfect habitat for the pink flamingo. Other common birds include kingfishers, cormorants, frigate birds, herons, egrets, white ibises, ospreys, hawks, and pelicans. For details on birdwatching tours in the lagoons, *see page 119.*

ENTERTAINMENT

Performing at Xcaret

Once the sun goes down, Cancún gears up. There's no shortage of places to go or things to do, and no need to take a long novel to fill those quiet moments – there just won't be any. Many people don't take to their beds until they've seen the sun come up. Before you head straight into the resort atmosphere of Cancún, check out what's happening in your hotel. Many have 'Las Vegas style' floor shows, Mexican evenings with traditional folk music and dances, and clubs where you can take to the dance floor yourself.

Cancún is developing so quickly that the latest hotspots change constantly. Ask your concierge where the place to be is, or just follow the crowds along the strip. Paseo Kukulcán in downtown Cancún has a collection of bars and clubs. On weekends you can join the locals in the Parque de Palapas, where the strains of rock, salsa, and folk music can blend together into a bewildering cacophony. But this doesn't prevent everyone from having great fun – and the atmosphere is definitely infectious.

If you choose to stay in Mujeres or Cozumel, things will be a bit more laid back. Cozumel has a number of music bars along Avenida Melgar and in the downtown region. All the large hotels have an entertainment program and a nightclub on site.

Fiestas

The Spanish colonists carried on the traditions of their mother country, and to this day there are yearly fiestas in most major

Dancing in Mérida

towns. Many mark saint's days or founding days, and the whole population will dress up and enjoy lots of singing and dancing. Most have a religious procession to start the proceedings. The major fiestas are listed in the Calendar of Events *(see page 94)*, but ask the tourist information office about what's going on during your stay.

The city of Mérida seems to be in the throes of a constant fiesta, hosting live cultural shows at sites around the downtown area. Here you will find the most authentic cultural displays in the region. The program changes nightly from ballet to traditional Yucatecan folk music and dances, and all the performances are free. There are special performances on the famed Mérida Domingos (Mérida Sundays), lasting all day except for a short break in the heat of the afternoon, and coinciding with a huge market. On Sunday evenings Mexican families take to the streets to meet friends and family, dance, and generally have a good time.

ATTRACTIONS FOR CHILDREN

Mexicans love children, and will dote on yours. Kids are always welcome in restaurants and cafés. There are also many attractions and activities in the region to keep them happy.

Beaches. Children can play for hours with sand and water. The beaches on the western coast of Cozumel offer crystal-clear, warm water with generally benign conditions and a range of amenities such as restaurants, restrooms, and lockers. Older children can enjoy snorkeling just offshore. Don't forget to protect young skin from the sun, which can be extremely powerful here. Always have a sun protection product at hand, and a layer of clothing such as a T-shirt. The sun's rays penetrate the water, so protection is needed when snorkeling also.

Submersible rides. Even very young children can safely see the fish and other marine life from inside a mini-submarine.

Boat trips. A day trip in a boat from Cancún to Isla Mujeres, or simply a trip around the coast or through the mangrove swamps can be a great adventure.

Dolphin Encounter. Older children can take to the water with these delightful marine mammals; younger children will enjoy watching the spectacle.

The Loltún Caves. These caves offer a relatively easy and safe introduction to the underground world. Some of the caverns are huge; the Maya artifacts make it even more interesting.

Xcaret. Superb beach, swimming lagoon, safe snorkeling, animals, horseback riding, turtles, underground river, Maya dances – what more would you need?

Calesa **rides at Mérida and Izamal**. Young and old alike enjoy touring the town in a small, horse-drawn buggy.

Fiesta celebrations. Youngsters will be very welcome at any Mexican celebration.

Wet'n Wild in Cancún. Water slides and wave machines for those who can't bear another moment at the beach!

Calendar of Events

January. *Año Nuevo* (New Year's Day): Religious festivals, parades, fireworks; new tribal leaders inaugurated throughout the Yucatán. *Three King's Day* is celebrated on the 6th.

February. *Carnival*: Week-long celebration leading up to Lent; parades, floats, dancing.

March. *Spring Equinox*, Chichén Itzá: Around the 21st, the spring sun aligns with the carved snake's head at the Temple of Kukulkán and fertilizes the earth for another year. *Easter*: The week before Easter is celebrated with reenactments of the events leading up to Christ's death. Processions and church services.

April. *Torneo Internacional de Pesca Deportiva*, Cozumel; Sport-fishing tournament takes place during the last week of the month.

May. *Labor Day*: Workers hold parades on the 1st. *Cedral Fair, Cozumel*: The anniversary of the first Catholic Mass celebrated in Mexico; cattle races and rides, bullfights held on the 1st–3rd. *Jazz Festival*, Cancún: dates vary.

June. *San Pedro y San Pablo*: Religious day of St Peter and St Paul; craft fairs and funfairs on the 29th.

September. *Fiesta de Independencia National* (Independence Day): National festival. *Fiestas de San Miguel Arcangel*: fiestas honoring the patron saint of Cozumel. *Fiesta del Señor de Las Ampollas* in Mérida (last week of September into October): Procession in the name of 'Christ of the Blisters.'

October. *Fiesta del Cristo de Sitilpech*: A figure of Christ is carried from Sitilpech almost to Izamal.

November. *Día de los Muertos/All Saints Day* and *All Souls Day*: National celebration of the dead on the 1st–2nd. *Cozumel Marathon* takes place early in the month. *Turneo de Pesca Día de la Revolucion Mexicana*, Cozumel: Revolution Day fishing tournament.

December. *Día de la Virgen de Guadalupe* (Day of the Virgin of Guadalupe): Religious processions followed by races. *Feast of the Immaculate Conception*, Izamal: Religious festivals and procession on the 3rd–9th.

EATING OUT

If you eat 'Mexican style,' you may have to turn your normal pattern upside down. *El desayuno* (breakfast) is generally served from 7am–11am, and *la cena* (dinner) from 7pm–10.30pm, while *la comida* (lunch), the main meal of the day, is a movable feast eaten any time between noon and 4pm, traditionally followed by a siesta. However, in the easy-going atmosphere of Cancún and the other resorts, any time is mealtime. Many restaurants are open all day (a few are open 24 hours), and you can easily find a place to eat any time between 7am and midnight. There are the ubiquitous fast-food outlets in Cancún and Cozumel, so you don't have to go without your favorite burger, though you probably won't miss it if you do. Tex-Mex and snack foods are also easy to find.

Breakfast

All hotels and most restaurants offer a choice of American, Continental, or Mexican-style breakfast – Mexicans eat a large breakfast, especially on Sundays. A breakfast favorite is *huevos a la Mexicana*, eggs scrambled with a mix of onion, tomato and chili peppers. *Huevos rancheros* are fried eggs on a bed of tortilla and refried beans with a tomato and chili sauce. Eggs also come scrambled with spicy sausage *(chorizo)*.

Classic Mexican Dishes

Mexican cuisine is the result of blending the indigenous Aztec and Maya culinary traditions with the Spanish and Middle-Eastern influences introduced by the conquistadors, and allowing the mixture to simmer for 400 years. You will find that the result is a rich and varied cuisine, far more exotic and exciting than you might expect, especially if you arrive with preconceptions based on your experience with Tex-Mex restaurants back home. In Mexico you will meet the flavors of coriander and cumin, chilies and bitter chocolate, tart, tangy limes and smooth, rich avocado.

But first, the basics. The staples of the Mexican kitchen are the same today as they were thousands of years ago when the native Indians first began to till the soil – corn, beans, and chilies.

Maíz, or corn, can be eaten on the cob (known as *elote*), but is principally used as cornmeal for making tortillas, the round, flat bread that accompanies almost every Mexican meal. Dried corn is boiled with lime to loosen the tough skin, then the cooked kernels are dried and ground into flour. The flour is mixed with a little water and patted out by expert hands into thin pancakes about 15cm (6in) in diameter.

Chicken being carved from the spit for tacos in Mérida; tacos also come filled with pork or beef

These days, a tortilla press does the job more quickly and efficiently, but you may still see women making tortillas by hand at market stalls and in tourist restaurants. The tortillas are cooked on a griddle, and served as an accompaniment or an integral part of the meal.

There are countless variations on the tortilla theme. *Tacos* are tortillas rolled around a filling of shredded barbecued pork, beef, or chicken, plus vegetables, and perhaps deep-fried. *Enchiladas* are stuffed tortillas smothered in sauce and baked. *Tostadas* are crisp, fried tortillas, topped with meat or fish and various sauces (*tostaditas* are quartered tortillas, deep-fried, and served with salsa and guacamole – you may know them as 'tortilla chips'). *Chilaquiles* are fried tortilla strips and meat filling layered in a casserole and baked. *Quesadillas* are tortillas topped with melted cheese (sometimes more) and served with refried beans.

> Enjoy your meal–
> *Buen provecho*
> (bwen proveycho)

Frijoles, or beans, are usually of the red kidney variety (though in the Yucatán they are black) and turn up in soups and stews. But you will come across them most often in the form of *frijoles refritos* (refried beans), a tasty accompaniment to most traditional Mexican dishes. Refried beans are made by boiling the beans until they are tender, then mashing them into a paste in a frying pan with sautéed onion, garlic, and chili.

The ingredient that usually first springs to mind when one thinks of Mexican cooking is the chili pepper. However, it is wrong to think that all Mexican food is stoked to a fiery heat with red-hot chilies – or indeed that all peppers are themselves hot. Peppers have been cultivated in Mexico since prehistoric times. Today there are estimated to be between 60 and 100 different varieties throughout the world, from the large, sweet red and green bell peppers in your local super-market to the tiny, excruciatingly hot *prik khii nuu* chilies from Thailand. Among the more common varieties you will experience in Mexico is the large, red, wrinkly *ancho*, with a rich, mild flavor, and the hotter *serrano*, which is smooth, green, and tapered. *Jalapeño* peppers are longer, thinner, and hotter than *serranos*, while the local Yucatecan pepper is the *habanero*, which is lantern-shaped, about 4cm (1½in) long, and can be green, yellow, or red, depending on how ripe it is. *Habaneros* have a rich, distinctive flavor and are fiery hot. The one to watch out for is the *chipotle* pepper, a dark red, wrinkly dried pepper used in the hottest of sauces.

Despite its reputation, Mexican food is generally not as piquant as you would expect. It is usually cooked with mild spices and served with a number of pepper or hot paprika sauces that you

Each restaurant makes its own sauces and strengths do vary – always test before adding one to your food!

then add to taste. No Mexican feast would be complete without a stack of warm tortillas and a dish or two of these sauces. *Salsa cruda* displays Mexico's national colors of red, white, and green in a blend of chopped tomato, onion, chili, and fresh cilantro (coriander), while *guacamole* is a delicious blend of finely chopped avocado, tomato, onion, garlic, chili, and cilantro. A local specialty is *Ixni-Pec* (a Maya phrase literally translated as the 'dog's nose' because it makes your nose wet), a very hot sauce made with *habanero* chiles, onion, tomato, and sour-orange juice. Beware – some of these sauces can be hot enough to make your tongue numb. A little certainly does go a long way.

Perhaps the most famous of all Mexican dishes, normally reserved for special occasions, is *mole poblano de Guajolote*, a stew of wild turkey in a richly flavored sauce of tomatoes, chilies, garlic, nuts, spices, and chocolate, which is reputed to have been served in the palace of Moctezuma, the Aztec emperor. Another classic is *pescado a la Veracruzana*, or fish Veracruz style. The fish is traditionally red snapper *(huachinango)*, or grouper *(mero)*, surrounded by a fragrant sauce of tomatoes, onions, capers, and olives, scented with cinnamon.

Specialties of Yucatán

The first surprise you may have after you arrive in Cancún is that your ideas about Mexican food will be radically altered. Mexico is such a big country that each of its regions has its own cuisine. The Yucatán is one of the more remote of these regions, and its cuisine has developed to create a number of unique dishes, combining Maya, Spanish, Caribbean and European influences. The countryside of the Puuc region is

As well as plain-grilled (below), fish can also be served with a sauce – Veracruz style

known as the 'garden of the Yucatán', producing delicious vegetables and fruit. The indigenous cuisine or *cocina típica* makes much use of local ingredients such as sour oranges, limes, cilantro, honey, and *habanero* chilies, along with onion and tomatoes that taste much more delicious than those at home. Any dish described as 'a la Yucateca' will have ingredients marinated or cooked in achiote, the ground seeds of the local annatto tree mixed into a paste with cumin seeds, garlic, peppercorns, and sour-orange juice.

Una cerveza – the perfect way to wash down a snack

Traditionally the people of the Yucatán have eaten chicken, turkey, and pork because, until recently, very few cattle were raised in the area. Today you can find beef on the menu, especially steak, which many say matches US beef in quality and taste. Filet mignon is available, but the most popular cut is *arrachera*, a skirt steak.

Classic Yucatecan dishes are *sopa de lima,* a hearty soup of chicken, vegetables, and crisp-fried tortilla strips flavored with lime juice; *pozole,* a thick stew of turkey and vegetables; *poc chuc*, thinly cut pork marinated in achiote paste; and *pollo ticuleño*, breaded chicken filet in tomato sauce, served with tortillas and beans and garnished with radish flowers, sliced bananas, and peas). *Pollo píbil* is chicken marinated in achiote paste and sour-orange sauce, baked in banana leaves; *píbil* means underground, and this dish was, until recently, cooked in earth ovens. The local people say it tastes much better cooked the traditional way, but today most restaurants slow-cook it in a normal oven. *Cochinita píbil* is pork cooked in the same way.

Some Yucatecan variations on the tortilla are *panuchos*, tortillas stuffed with black-bean paste, fried, and topped with chicken, onion, and tomato; *salbutes*, tortillas topped with shredded chicken or turkey; and *papadzules*, tortillas stuffed with hard-boiled egg with a sauce of tomato and onion spiked with chili and ground pumpkin seeds. You will also find *tamales*, cornmeal steamed in banana leaves, which can be either savory, with chicken or turkey meat and tomato sauce, or sweet, with sugar or fruit compote.

Don't miss the chance to sample the succulent Caribbean seafood. Fish in all varieties is served plain grilled or breaded. Shark meat is very popular in the Yucatán, and is stewed or cut into steaks. *Langosta* (lobster) and *camarónes* (shrimp) are delicious simply grilled, or fried and served with garlic sauce. Conch (an abalone-like shellfish), shrimp, and whitefish, marinated and partially cooked by the acidity of lime juice, then seasoned with tomato, onion, chili, and coriander, are the components of the popular appetizer called *ceviche*.

The usual way to round off dinner is with a platter of fresh, tropical fruit: sweet, juicy pineapple, refreshing papaya and melon, succulent mango and banana, and tangy orange. For something more filling, try *arroz con leche* (rice pudding with raisins) or *flan* (crème caramel).

Drinks

Mexican beer *(cerveza)* is excellent, and is exported all over the world. It comes in two varieties, light *(clara)* and dark *(negra)*, and has a higher alcoholic content than most North American beers. Labels to choose include Bohemia, Dos

Equis, Sol, and Corona. When chilled they are perfect for quenching one's thirst on a hot sunny day. You will find them served with a piece of lime, which imparts a slight 'tang' to the overall taste. Dark beers have a nuttier, fuller taste, but are also served chilled.

If you want to try locally produced beer, a brewery in Mérida produces a range that you can find in most establishments along the coast. They include the dark Leon brand and the light Montejo brand.

Imported wines are available in the better restaurants, but Mexican wine, from the vineyards of Baja in the northwest of the country, is well worth trying.

The national liquor is tequila, a fiery spirit distilled from the fermented juice of the agave plant. It is traditionally knocked back neat, accompanied by a pinch of salt and a twist of lime, or sipped slowly in a margarita, a cocktail of tequila, triple sec, lime juice, and crushed ice served in a salt-rimmed glass. Another popular cocktail is the tequila sunrise, a colorful concoction of tequila, crème de cassis, lime juice, and grenadine.

Mezcal is a regional variation of tequila distinguished by the presence of a pickled *agave* worm at the bottom of the

Jugos y Licuados

Probably the most tempting drinks the Yucatán has to offer are its fresh fruit juices *(jugos),* including orange, mango, melon, papaya, grapefruit, and pineapple. A variation for the non-citrus fruits are the *licuados* (milk shakes), with mango, pineapple, and banana being the most popular. Juices and *licuados* are available at most restaurants, but there are also juice bars. For a truly mouthwatering choice, try Janitzio on Mérida's Plaza Grande, which also specializes in fresh fruit ices and sorbets.

You can choose from the wide variety of tequilas, Mexico's national liquor

bottle. The worm was traditionally added as a sign of quality – if the Mezcal was good the worm would stay intact, but if it was of poor quality the worm would rot in the bottle. Although there is no longer a need for this quality control mechanism, the worm stays by popular demand.

Kahlúa is a pleasant coffee-flavored Mexican liqueur, but a more exotic after-dinner drink is *xtabentún*, a Maya liqueur flavored with fermented honey, flower petals, and anise.

Familiar brands of soft drinks *(refrescos)* are bottled under license in Mexico and are available everywhere, as is mineral water. For a delicious alternative to carbonated drinks, try freshly prepared juices and shakes *(see opposite)*. The Yucatecans use corn to make *atole*, a non-alcoholic drink. Another beverage originating from the Yucatán is *horchata*, a concentrated rice, almond, and coconut mixture to which you add water to taste.

Coffee is usually served black; if you want it with milk ask for *café con leche*. A spicy Mexican variation is *café de olla*, which is coffee brewed in a small earthenware pot (the olla) with cinnamon, cloves, and hard brown sugar *(poncillo)*. *Té de manzanilla*, chamomile tea, is a refreshing change from coffee, and is known to be particularly good for settling an upset stomach. Some establishments will still serve *chaya* drinks, made from a vegetable like spinach used by the Maya in healing. You can take it as tea or mixed with lemonade as a cold drink.

To Help You Order...

Here are some select terms that will enhance your dining experience. Be bold and try to scrape by in Spanish – your efforts will be appreciated.

Do you have a table for one/two/three/four people?	**¿Tiene una mesa para una/dos/tres/cuatro persona/personas?**
Do you have a menu?	**¿Tiene un menú?**
The bill, please.	**La cuenta, por favor.**

...And Read the Menu

aguacate	avocado	**frijoles**	beans
ajo	garlic	**huevos**	eggs
albahaca	basil	**leche**	milk
bistek	steak	**mantequilla**	butter
café	coffee	**mariscos**	seafood
calamares	squid	**mejillones**	mussels
camarones	shrimp	**papas**	potatoes
cerdo/puerco	pork	**pescado**	fish
cerveza	beer	**pollo**	chicken
ensalada	salad	**queso**	cheese
flan	sweet custard	**sopa**	soup

HANDY TRAVEL TIPS

An A–Z Summary of Practical Information

Note that the peso is signified by the $ sign, prices quoted in dollars by US$.

A

ACCOMMODATIONS (see also CAMPING, and the list of Recommended Hotels on page 129)

The first hotels in the Tourist Zone of Cancún did not appear until the early 1970s, and the proliferation of building since that time has seen over 120 hotels completed and more being planned. Because the resorts are so new, the hotels are all equipped to a very high standard, and accommodations of a lower quality are not available. All rooms have in-suite cable and air-conditioning, and have a range of guest amenities such as pools, spas, and gyms, equipment for numerous watersports, and a number of golf courses. In some hotels these activities will be included in the price, though this is something you will need to confirm before you make a reservation. In downtown Cancún, you will find lower priced establishments and business-type hotels. These are a short car or bus journey from the beaches and will usually have basic, clean facilities.

On Cozumel and Isla Mujeres and along the coast of the Maya Riviera, there is a much wider range of accommodations. There are a few luxury hotels, but also many mid-range options and smaller, family-run hotels.

The high season in the resorts runs from December through April, the off season from May through December. Prices can vary by as much as 50 percent between high and low seasons. It is important to make a firm reservation if you intend to travel in high season.

In the countryside of the Yucatán, a number of old haciendas (plantation houses) have been transformed into hotels. Some market themselves as exclusive hideaways and can be expensive, but they do offer a unique experience to guests. Mérida has a range of hotels, with many good budget options and a number with luxury ratings.

You will find accommodations at all major Maya sites, but it can be expensive. Always book in advance if you intend to say overnight, particularly in high season, as group bookings can completely fill hotels.

A 10 percent tax is added to prices in Cancún: this may or may not be quoted in the price, so always ask when you are given a room rate whether tax is included.

I'd like a single/double room	**Quisiera una habitación sencilla/doble**
with bath/shower	**con baño/regadera**
What's the rate per night?	**¿Cuál es el precio por noche?**
Where is there a budget hotel?	**¿Dónde hay un hotel económico?**

AIRPORTS *(aeropuertos)* (See also GETTING THERE)

Cancún International Airport, 20km (12 miles) south of the city, is the second busiest airport in Mexico. It is a domestic airport, serves the resort (which has almost 3 million visitors each year) with international scheduled and charter flights, and acts as the feeder airport for many of the northern Maya archaeological sites. Facilities include a tourist information office, car rental agencies, duty-free stores, and restaurants and bars.

Your hotel may have a courtesy bus to pick you up at the airport; otherwise you can take a minibus *(colectivo)* to either the Hotel Zone or downtown. They run every 30 minutes during the day. Buy your tickets at a kiosk in the 'arrivals' area; the fare is around US$10. The minibus does not operate a return service so you will need to take a taxi back to the airport at departure time. Taxi fares are around US$30–40 depending on the exact location of your hotel.

A departure tax is levied on all flights. This is usually included in the price of the ticket, but do check with your travel agent. If it is not included, the tax must be paid on departure in cash (either US dollars or pesos).

If you intend to travel from the airport to Isla Mujeres by boat, you will need transportation to the Puerto Juárez passenger ferry. A taxi is the direct but expensive option. The minibus will take you to the bus station in downtown Cancún, where you can take another to the passenger jetty.

Cozumel has an international airport just 5 minutes north of San Miguel. It takes direct flights from destinations in the US, as well as onward flights from Cancún, Mérida, and Mexico City. A *colectivo* from the airport into town will cost $6; taxis are roughly twice as much.

Mérida airport has few international flights but a busy domestic schedule, with regular flights to and from Cancún and Cozumel.

B

BUDGETING FOR YOUR TRIP

Prices in the resort areas of Cancún and Cozumel are generally higher than resorts in the US, but represent good value when compared with the UK and Europe. If you make a hotel booking as an individual, most rates will be quoted as European plan (just room), but you should be able to book American plan (room and meals) if you want. Some hotels operate an all-inclusive policy; one price covers room, food, drinks, and activities.

Archaeological sites. The entrance fee to most Maya sites is $20–30, though Chichén Itzá and Uxmal are considerably more expensive ($100), but the fee includes the sound-and-light shows. Children under 12 are almost always admitted for free, but only Mexicans have free admission on Sundays.

Ecoparks. The ecopark attractions range from around US$25 (Xel-Ha) to US$50 (Xcaret) per person per day; children half-price.

Other Activities. 'Swimming with Dolphins' programs can cost up to US$150; two tank dive US$70; snorkel rental US$8; jungle tour on speedboat in the lagoon US$30; 30 minutes horseback riding US$20.

Bus. Hotel Zone to El Centro (downtown Cancún) $5; Cancún to Playa del Carmen $35.

Car rental. US$90 per day, less in low season.

Ferry. Playa del Carmen to Cozumel US$15 round-trip; Cancún to Isla Mujeres $35 single from Puerto Juaréz, US$15 from the Hotel Zone.

Meals. Dinner for one at a mid-priced restaurant US$30–40

Taxi. Hotel Zone to downtown US$10.

Once out in the Yucatán – away from the main tourist areas – prices for most goods drop dramatically.

C

CAMPING

There are few opportunities for camping in the Yucatán, though RV parks can be found near Uxmal and Chichén Itzá, as well as along the coast around Playa del Carmen.

CAR RENTAL *(coches de alquiler)* (See also DRIVING)

Car rental in Mexico is expensive by international standards, but it is a good option if you intend to travel around the Yucatán from Cancún. Roads are generally in good condition and traffic light – except in the downtown areas. Although there are many tours to the major archaeological sites, having your own vehicle will free you to explore the lands of the Maya on your own time. It would not be wise to drive at night in the countryside, because the roads are rarely lit and animals do stray across them.

You will need to hold a current valid driver's license and be over 21 (25 for some agencies). National driver's licenses from all major countries are accepted when renting a vehicle. If you do not have a credit card, you will be required to pay a large cash deposit.

All the major international car rental agencies operate from Cancún International Airport (or Cozumel Airport), or you can take delivery at your hotel.

Prices start from around US$70 per day for a GM Chevy Pop. This includes tax but not insurance, which runs around $15 per day. It pays to shop around. Watch out for terms of insurance – excess charges on fully comprehensive cover, for instance. You may get a better rate by the week and by pre-booking your rental car before you arrive in Cancún. Be aware that if you make a booking while in the resort, you will be given a quote in US dollars but charged in pesos – at whatever exchange rate the company deems appropriate. If you rent for more than a few days, this practice could give you a nasty shock when you get your credit card bill.

Make a note of the telephone number of your car rental office just in case you break down. You can call them to arrange assistance. Exploring Cozumel is greatly benefited by having a vehicle of some kind, even if only for a couple of days. Prices are similar to those at Cancún, as are the rules governing vehicle rental.

Here are contact telephone numbers for the major car rental agencies. **Avis** in Cancún; tel: 998/886-0238, or (800) 331-1212 (toll-free). **Budget** in Cancún; tel: 998/884-5011, in Cozumel; tel: 987/872-0903, or (800) 527-0700 (toll-free). **Dollar** in Cancún; tel: 998/886-0159. **Hertz** in Cancún; tel: 998/884-4692. Other companies to look out for are **Executive**, **National** and **Localiza**.

Exploring Isla Mujeres is fun, but the island is too small to warrant car rental. Alternative forms of transportation include: golf cart rental on Mujeres US$50 per day; moto (motor-scooter) US$30 per day; bicycle $5 per day.

CLIMATE

The Yucatán has a tropical climate; the temperature remains fairly constant throughout the year, rarely falling below 27°C (81°F) during the day. Expect them to reach around 33°C (92°F).

The year is split into two 'seasons': the dry, between December and mid-May, roughly coincides with the peak tourist season; the rainy, between mid-May and November, sees increased humidity but no decrease in temperature. Hurricane season falls between July and early November, and Cancún experiences a small number of tropical storms each year, though there is no regular pattern. These storms are generally well forecast by meteorological scientists.

The following chart lists the average temperature for each month:

	J	F	M	A	M	J	J	A	S	O	N	D
°C	21	21	22	24	26	27	28	29	27	26	23	21
°F	70	70	72	75	79	81	82	84	81	79	73	70

CLOTHING

Cool and casual are the bywords for your trip to Cancún and Cozumel. During the day you will need only beachware, T-shirts, and shorts for all the resort areas. Natural fabrics such as cotton and silk are the most comfortable in hot, humid climates. Sunglasses are important, especially on the beaches, where the pale sand reflects the sun's strong light. If you intend to travel inland to the towns and villages, and especially if you wish to enter churches, you should dress more conservatively. Always take a covering layer and a hat for archaeological sites – to avoid taking too much sun – and don't forget comfortable footwear for climbing the temple steps.

As the sun sets, the mood remains casual – ties and jackets are rarely needed – but most people change into something informal or 'tropical' for dinner. A light sweater may come in handy for the odd cooler evening.

CRIME AND SAFETY (See also POLICE)

Generally, the Yucatán is a relatively safe place to visit, but still prone to some petty crime directed against tourists in and around the resort areas. Always watch your luggage at airports, getting into taxis, and checking in and out of hotels. Use the hotel safe for all valuables, and do not leave anything on view in your rental vehicle. When sunbathing, don't leave valuables to go swimming. Report any theft to the police immediately. Keep to well-lit public areas after dark.

You will find specially trained 'tourist police' patrolling the streets of the city centers in Mérida and Izamal. You will be able to go to them with any problems or difficulties that you may have; they all speak some English.

CUSTOMS (*aduana*) AND ENTRY REQUIREMENTS

American and Canadian visitors can enter Mexico with their passport or birth certificate accompanied by a photo ID. Visitors from other countries normally only require a passport valid for at least six months.

Though you don't need a visa, each traveler must carry a Mexican Tourist Permit while in the country. Tourist permits are issued by the airlines, cruise companies, and at border crossings, and are normally valid for 30 days but can cover periods of up to 180 days. Always make sure that your stamp covers the length of your stay.

Customs officials will want to be sure that you are not bringing goods to sell while you are in Mexico. Those with a large amount of luggage or unusual pieces are likely to be searched and questioned, but items such as golf clubs, scuba gear, and camera equipment should be fine. You are also allowed to bring in 400 cigarettes or 50 cigars, and 1kg (2.2lbs) of tobacco, 2 1-liter bottles of alcohol (any strength), and 12 rolls of film into the country.

Currency restrictions. Non-residents may import or export any amount of freely convertible foreign currency into Mexico, provided that it is declared on arrival. There is no limit to the amount of Mexican currency you may carry into or out of Mexico.

| I have nothing to declare. | **Yo tengo nada que declarar.** |

D

DRIVING

In Mexico, drive on the right and pass on the left. The US Department of State issues a pamphlet entitled *Tips for Travelers to Mexico* available for US$1 from Superintendent of Documents, US Government Printing Office, Washington, DC 20401.

Road conditions are not generally as good as those found in the US or Europe, though they are perfectly adequate and always improving. Roads in the Cancún area are good; the major connecting highways down the coast to Tulum and across to Mérida are too. There is a toll road, the 180, from Cancún to Mérida (tolls are relatively high, so the highway is quiet), but it bypasses many settlements that offer fascinating insight into the lifestyle of the local people.

In Cancún, traffic is controlled by traffic lights at intersections, but there are a number of traffic circles as well. Right of way goes to traffic already on the rotary.

Built-up areas and villages in the countryside have speed control devices, usually *topes*, speed bumps. There are also *topes* in downtown Cancún, marking the main pedestrian crossings on Avenida Tulum.

The narrow streets of San Miguel de Cozumel have their own set of rules. If you are traveling parallel to the sea, you have the right of way at all junctions. Those traveling east–west do not have right of way and should stop at every intersection. However, this is not general knowledge to visitors – so take extra care!

Rules and regulations. Speed limits are 30–40km/h (19–25mph) in towns, 60km/h (38mph) in the Hotel Zone, and 110km/h (69mph) on the toll road out of town. There is an unwritten rule in Mexico that drivers wishing to turn left across traffic should pull off the highway to the right if they have traffic behind them, and allow it to pass before they turn rather than slow and block the highway.

Fuel costs. Pemex (Petroleras Mexicanas), a government-controlled company, has a monopoly on gas *(gasolina)* sales. They do not accept credit cards in payment. Gas is sold by the liter in regular *(nova)*, super *(extra)*, and lead-free *(magna sin)*. If traveling in the countryside, do anticipate your gas needs, as stations are few and far-between once out of the major settlements. The only fuel stations on Cozumel are in San Miguel.

Parking. Do not park where you see red lines on the kerb, or where there is a sign of an 'E' with a line through it. Most hotels have parking lots, but some charge for them. This is especially true in Mérida.

Road signs. Mexican road signs are the standard international pictographs, but you may also encounter these written signs.

Alto	Stop
Ceda el paso	Give way
Circulación	Direction of traffic
Cruce de peatones	Pedestrian crossing
Curva peligrosa	Dangerous bend
Cuidado	Caution
Cuota	Toll
Desviacion	Detour
Disminuya su velocidad	Reduce speed
Escuela	School
Peligro	Danger
Prohibido estacionarse	No parking
Prohibido rebasar	No overtaking
Salida de camiones	Truck exit

(International) driver's license	**Licencia para manejar (internacional)**
Car registration papers	**registro del automóvil**
Are we on the right road for…?	**¿Es ésta la carretera hacia…?**
Fill the tank, top grade, please.	**Llénelo, por favor, con super.**
Check the oil/tires/battery.	**Revise el aceite/las llantas/ la batería.**
I've broken down.	**Mi carro se ha descompuesto.**
There's been an accident.	**Ha habido un accidente.**
Could you mend this flat?	**¿Puede arreglar este pinchazo?**

Bringing your car into Mexico. Although the Yucatán is a long way from the northern Mexican border, you may want to travel across country with your own vehicle or RV. The following guidelines apply: You will need a temporary importation permit, which can be obtained at any border crossing. This must be surrendered when you leave Mexico. A car importation fee must be paid by credit card (in the same name as the vehicle registration document). Car registration documents must be carried, along with a valid driver's license. You must sign a form promising to leave the country with your vehicle.

If you need further help or information, contact AAA.

If you need help. A government-sponsored highway patrol, the *Angeles Verdes* (Green Angels), patrol the major highways twice each day between 8am–8pm. They offer free roadside assistance (though you will have to pay for parts) as well as information, and they speak English. They can be contacted at (800) 903-0092 (toll-free). You should also take the telephone number of your car rental office or an associated breakdown business, since they will be able to help in case of difficulty. If you do have a breakdown, try to take your vehicle off the highway while waiting for assistance.

E

ELECTRICITY *(corriente eléctrica)*

Mexico uses the 120V/60Hz system, the same as the US and Canada. Travelers from other countries will need an adapter for their appliances – buy one at home rather than waiting until you arrive.

EMBASSIES AND CONSULATES *(embajadas y consulados)*

There are consulates in Cancún for the following countries:

Canada: Centro Comercial de Mexico, Loco 312, 200 Avenida Tulum (Downtown), 77500 Cancún, tel: 998/884-3716.

US: Plaza Caracol, 3rd floor, #320-323, km 8.5 Boulevard Kukulcán (Hotel Zone), 77500 Cancún, tel: 998/883-0272.

UK: street address Boulevard Kukulcán, km 17 lot 50 (Hotel Zone); postal address PO Box 105, Boulevard Kukulcán, 77500 Cancún, tel: 998/885-1166.

Otherwise, the nearest consular contact in Mexico is in Mexico City.

Australia: Plaza Polanco, Jaime Balmes #11, B-Tower 10th floor, Colonia Polanco, Mexico D.F. 11510, tel: (525) 395-9988; fax: (525) 395-7870.

Canada: Avenida Schillar #529, Colonia Chapultepec Polanco, Mexico D.F. 11560, tel: (525) 724-7900.

New Zealand: J L Legrange #103, 10th floor, Colonia Los Morales Polanco, Mexico D.F. 11510, tel: (525) 281-5486; fax: (525) 281-5212.

UK: Rio Lerman #71, Colonia Cuauhtémoc, Mexico D.F. 06500, tel: (525) 207-2089; fax: (525) 207-7672.

US: Paseo de la Reforma #305, Colonia Cuauhtémoc, Mexico D.F. 06500, tel: (525) 211-0042.

Citizens of South Africa and Ireland do not have representation, and should contact the British or US embassy in case of difficulty.

EMERGENCIES *(emergencias)* (See also POLICE)

The emergency telephone number (similar to 911 in the US or 999 in the UK) is 060, but there are also separate telephone numbers for each emergency service in each town. It would help to have a Spanish speaker with you when you make the call; otherwise enlist the help of your hotel receptionist or tourist information office.

Police *(policía)*: Cancún tel: 998/884-1913; Cozumel tel: 987/872-0409

G

GAY AND LESBIAN TRAVELERS

Mexico is a conservative country with a deep Catholic faith. Because of this, overt displays of affection between the same sex are not seen within society and would be regarded as shocking. However, there is no undercurrent of harassment within society and gay individuals should have no concerns about visiting the Yucatán.

GETTING THERE

By Air
Cancún. From North America there are many daily connections to hubs or directly to Cancún. Try the following airlines by phone or on the Internet (all numbers are toll-free in the US): US Airways (tel: 800/428-4322; <www.usairways.com>); United Airlines (tel: 800/241-6522; <www.ual.com>); American Airlines (tel: 800/443-7300; <www.aa.com>); Continental (tel: 800/231-0856; <www.flycontinental.com>); Mexicana (tel: 800/531-7921; <www.mexicana.com/g4mx/main/Main/>); Aeromexico (tel: 800/237-6639; <www.aeromexico.com>). Package plans (flights/hotel/meals for one

price) from a number of companies offer big savings compared to making separate arrangements for each element of your vacation. The range of options is huge, so take your time to compare them and consult a travel agent if necessary. Several airlines offer packages in addition to flights. Try Aeromexico Vacations (tel: 800/245-8585; <www.aeromexicovacations.com>) and American Airlines Vacations (tel: 800/321-2121; <aav7.aavacations.com>).

The choice of direct, non-stop flights from the UK is limited to package tour operators such as MyTravel and First Choice. However, there are other options, including with Martinair (<www.martinair.com>) from Amsterdam (booked from London through KLM – <www. klm.com>) and Iberia (<www.iberia.es>) from London via Madrid to Cancún. Alternatively, Cancún can be reached via Miami, Dallas/Fort Worth or Mexico City and an onward connecting flight. From South Africa and Australia/New Zealand, you will find the most sensible connections would be through a US airport with onward flight to Cancún.

Travelers heading for Cozumel, Playa del Carmen, or Mérida transfer to local carriers like Aerocaribe (<www.aerocaribe.com>) at Cancún. It is usually less expensive to book the onward internal flight together with your main flight.

By Boat

Those who fly to Cancún and do not wish to connect to Cozumel by plane must take the land route to Playa del Carmen and transfer by ferry. This 40–50 minute trip leaves every hour from 5am–11pm (the Playa del Carmen to Cozumel route). The bus service from Cancún to the passenger jetty in Playa del Carmen is regular, reliable, and inexpensive. The main bus station in Cancún is on Avenida Tulum.

A number of cruise lines make stops at Cozumel, with trips to the surrounding Maya sites. The main departure points are Miami and Puerto Rico. Carnival and Celebrity cruise lines are among the major companies offering a Cozumel stop.

GUIDES AND TOURS *(guías; visitas guidas)*

Though you will not need a guide in the resort areas, it will be helpful to have one at the archaeological sites; all the major sites will have English-speaking guides waiting at the entrance to offer their services.

There are a number of commercial companies organizing morning or day tours to sites around Cancún and Cozumel. Tours may include lunch and a guide and offer a chance to swim or snorkel in addition to seeing the temples. From Isla Mujeres you can take tours with a number of operators to Isla Contoy for a day of snorkeling. There are also birdwatching tours of the coastal mangrove lagoons at Celestún and Río Lagartos. At Celestún contact the Cultur visitors' center for birdwatching tours; at Río Lagartos, which is less developed, it's best to go with recognized guides such as Diego Martínez and Ismael Navarro, who are based at the Restaurant Isla Contoy (tel: 986 862-0000, www.ismaelnavarro.gobot.com). Tours are available locally at the village of Punta Allen at the end of the very bumpy Boca Paila road south of Tulum, for exploration of the Sian Ka'an Biosphere Reserve. Contact Amigos de Sian Ka'an in Cancún (tel: 998 884-9583) for further details.

We'd like an English-speaking guide.	**Queremos un guía que hable inglés.**
I need an English interpreter.	**Necesito un intérprete de inglés.**

H

HEALTH AND MEDICAL CARE

There are no immediate health concerns to worry about before your trip to the Yucatán. Always take out adequate insurance to cover emergency health problems, repatriation, or hospital treatment.

You will not need any inoculations unless you have traveled from a risk area to reach Mexico. However, if you intend to tour farther south into Belize or Guatemala, you should take advice from your doctor. Mosquitoes are a problem. Always carry insect repellent and apply it regularly when you visit the archaeological sites, and after dark no matter where you are.

There are numerous English-speaking doctors and medical facilities in Cancún, Cozumel, and along the Maya Riviera, so if there is a problem you should have no difficulty finding help. Your hotel will always have the services of an English-speaking doctor on hand. There are good hospitals in Cancún (Hospital Americano, tel: 998/884-6133) and in Mérida (Centro Médico de la Americas, tel: 999/927-3199).You should have no problem obtaining most over-the-counter drugs – you'll find pharmacies in large supermarkets and town centers.

The risks of stomach upsets is nowhere near as great as it used to be. Times have moved on and the water you are served at a restaurant or the ice that goes in your juice or *licuado* is all *agua purificada* (purified water), and thus perfectly safe. Salads are prepared using *agua purificada*, so they, too, are safe. This applies not just to Cancún, but all towns with a restaurant trade. There may be the odd exception that proves the rule, and you shouldn't push your luck with roadside juice sellers, for example, but the days of 'Montezuma's revenge' are almost gone. If you do become ill, take plenty of fluids with a little salt and sugar to avoid dehydration and contact a doctor.

The sun of the Yucatán is hot and strong, and in Cancún the sand reflects a great deal of heat and light. Always limit your time in the sun for the first few days to avoid sunburn, and apply a sun protection product regularly. Carry a covering layer (a long-sleeved shirt perhaps) that you can put on if you can't find any shade. Always wear a hat and sunglasses to avoid damage to the eyes. Be particularly careful with children's skin – always keep it protected with clothing or a sunblock product.

L

LANGUAGE

The official language of Mexico is Spanish, though a slightly different dialect than that spoken in Spain. Some 10 pecent of the population speak an indigenous Indian language, and you will find that in the countryside of the Yucatán many people will speak the native Maya language.

English is understood and spoken by the vast majority of people in the tourist areas, though they will still undoubtedly welcome any attempts by visitors to speak Spanish. You will find some basic Latin-American Spanish phrases throughout this book, but for more comprehensive help, the *Berlitz Latin-American Spanish for Travelers* phrase book covers most situations you are likely to encounter.

M

MAPS

If you intend to stay around the Hotel Zone in Cancún, or on Cozumel or Mujeres, you will find maps at the local tourist offices. For touring out of the resort areas, you will need more detailed information. AAA produces comprehensive maps of the Yucatán region.

MEDIA

The News is Mexico's English-language daily. Published in Mexico City, it can be found at major newsstands in the region. Major US newspapers can be purchased in all the resort areas, along with some European papers in Playa de Carmen, though these are generally a day old.

Most large hotels will have satellite or cable TV with major US channels such as CNN and ESPN.

MONEY *(moneda)*

Currency. The unit of currency in Mexico is the peso, denoted by a $ sign. US dollars are accepted at most businesses in the tourist areas. To avoid confusion between the US$ and the peso, most stores and restaurants in the tourist areas will quote US dollar prices with the abbreviation 'Dlls' or 'USD.' When buying goods in markets, etc., always make sure that you know whether you are negotiating in US dollars or Mexican pesos.

Peso notes are printed in the following denominations: $20, 50, 100, 200, 500. Coins are $1, 2, 5, 10, 20. Each peso is split into 100 *centavos*, though these are not generally found in cities or tourist resorts. However, if you travel to country markets and small settlements, these smaller coins are still in circulation; you will find them in denominations of 5, 10, 20, and 50c. Small change is always in short supply in Mexico, so keep any you come across.

Currency exchange. Currency can be exchanged at a number of places, with the best rates available at banks. Opening hours have expanded lately to about 9am–5pm Monday–Friday and 9am–noon on Saturdays, though you may not find them open when you expect to. The commercial tourist exchange houses *(casas de cambio)* are open longer hours than banks but may offer a less advantageous rate. Airports also have currency exchange kiosks, but these offer the lowest rates.

Credit cards *(tarjetas de crédito)*. Credit cards are widely accepted in shops, restaurants, and at attractions in the main resorts. Outside these areas always ask whether they are accepted. Gas stations only deal in cash.

ATMs. The easiest (and least costly) way of obtaining local currency is by using an ATM machine with your debit/credit card. Any major bank such as Banamex, found in most towns, will have an ATM inside; machines are also strategically located in Cancún's shopping plazas. Some machines in Cancún and Cozumel issue pesos and US dollars.

Travelers' checks *(cheque de viajero)*. Travelers' checks can be cashed at banks and exchange kiosks (take your passport as ID), though there will be a charge for the service. They are also widely accepted in stores and restaurants in the main tourist areas.

I want to change some dollars/pounds.	**Quiero cambiar dólares/libras.**
Do you accept travelers' checks?	**¿Acepta usted cheques de viajero?**
Can I pay with this credit card?	**¿Puedo pagar con esta tarjeta de crédito?**
How much does it cost?	**¿Cuánto es?**
Do you have anything less expensive?	**¿Tiene algo más barato?**

O

OPEN HOURS

Archaeological sites are generally open daily from 8am–5pm, though some are open shorter hours on Sundays. Government offices are open from 9am–5pm, probably longer if they deal with visitors, and though the siesta has disappeared in the resort area, you may still find the person you need to speak to is absent from 2pm–4pm. They will make up their hours by working later into the evening.

Stores in tourist areas are generally open until 9pm. Car rental and tour operator offices open at 9am and close between 7pm and 9pm.

P

POLICE *(policía)*

The police have a checkered reputation throughout Mexico, but their image is more positive in the tourist areas of the Yucatán. Police wear brown and beige uniforms; you can find them patrolling the Hotel Zone and downtown in Cancún, Cozumel, and central Mérida. The main police station in Cancún is on Avenida Tulum, next to the tourist office. In the Hotel Zone there is a smaller office near the Sheraton Hotel. Mérida also has a 'tourist police' force patrolling the downtown area. They speak English and wear light beige pants in contrast to the brown pants of the normal police force.

If you need to report a theft or crime and your Spanish isn't strong, try to have a Spanish speaker with you. The emergency number to call for the police is 060.

I've lost my wallet/ purse/passport.	**He perdido mi cartera/ bolsa/pasaporte.**

POST OFFICES (*correos*)

The main post office in Cancún is on Avenida Sunyaxchén; open Monday–Friday 8am–7pm, Saturday 9am–1pm. In Cozumel, the main post office is Avenida Melgar a few minutes south of the pier; open Monday–Friday 9am–1pm and 3pm–6pm, Saturday 9am–1pm.

Stamps (*estampillas, timbres*) can be bought at newsagents or drugstores. When you buy your postcards ask if you can buy stamps at the same time. Mailboxes are blue and gray. Most hotels will post cards for you, so ask at reception. The postal service is extremely slow, often 14 days to North America and longer to Europe. If you have anything that is urgent or valuable, it would be better to send it by commercial carrier.

PUBLIC HOLIDAYS (*dias festivos*)

National holidays fall on the following dates.

January 1	*Año Nuevo*	(New Years Day)
February 5	*Aniversario de la Constitución*	(Constitution Day)
March 21	*Nacimiento de Benito Juárez*	(Juárez's birthday)

Variable	*Pascua, Semana Santa* (Easter, Holy Week)
May 1	*Día del Trabajo* (Labor Day)
May 5	*Batalla de Puebla* (Anniversary of the Battle of Puebla)
September 1	*Informe presidencial* (First Day of Congress)
September 16	*Día de la Independencia* (Independence Day)
October 12	*Día de la Raza* (Columbus Day/Day of the Race)
November 2	*Día de los Muertos* (Day of the Dead)
November 20	*Aniversario de la Revolucion* (Anniversary of the Revolution)
December 12	*Día de Nuestra Señora de Guadalupe* (Day of Our Lady of Guadalupe)
December 25	*Navidad* (Christmas Day)

PUBLIC TRANSPORTATION *(transporte publico)*

Buses. In Cancún, a regular bus service runs through the Hotel Zone to downtown and back for $5. Long-distance buses that run down the coast to Playa del Carmen and Tulum, or west to Mérida, depart from the bus station on Avenida Tulum at Avenida Uxmal. Prices are very inexpensive: the fare with the Riviera bus company from Cancún to Playa del Carmen is around $35.

What is the fare for…?   **Cuál es la tarifa a…?**

Taxis. Taxis are numerous along the Zona Turística in Cancún – they are green-and-white and will sound their horn as they drive past. You can hail them on the street, or your hotel will call one for you. Fares for each journey are pre-set – ask your hotel reception or local tourist information office how much it should be. In Cozumel taxis can be found outside the main pier – where a list of standard fares is posted – and at the cruise ports. Taxis can also be hired by the morning or day if you want to see the sights. Always agree on a price before setting out. If you are in a group of several people, it may be less expensive to take a taxi for the day than to book bus tours.

Ferries. Frequent ferry services run from Puerto Juárez (10 minutes from downtown Cancún) to Isla Mujeres. There are crossings every half hour, with the last one leaving Mujeres at 7.30pm. Less frequent and more expensive services run from Playa Linda Marine Terminal and Playa Caracol to Mujeres, but these may not run out of season.

Ferries to Cozumel from the mainland run from Playa del Carmen, with several crossings per day. A car ferry service is also available from Puerto Morelos.

R

RELIGION

Mexico is a predominantly Roman Catholic country and the population still worships regularly. Always dress conservatively when entering a Catholic place of worship.

T

TELEPHONE *(teléfonos)*

The international dialing code for Mexico is 52, preceded by 011 if calling from the US or Canada; 00 if calling from the UK. All area codes are now 3-digit, followed by a 7-digit number. If dialing within the area, there is no need to dial the code. The easiest way of calling locally or internationally is to use a Telmex phonecard, available for $30, $50 and $100 at most groceries and newsagents and usable at the ubiquitous Ladatel payphones. Most large hotels will have direct-dial facilities for local and international calls, but this is always more expensive than using a phonecard or credit cards.

International dialing codes are as follows (always prefix these codes with 00): US and Canada 1; UK 44; Australia 61; New Zealand 64; South Africa 27; Ireland 353.

TIME ZONES

The Yucatán operates in the same time zone as US Central Standard Time, 6 hrs behind GMT, but does not change to daylight saving in the summer.

Yucatán noon	New York 1pm	London 6pm	Johannesburg 6pm	Sydney 3am

TIPPING *(propina; servicio)*

Service charges are not generally included in the final check in hotels and restaurants and, because wages are low in Mexico, service personnel rely on money earned in tips. Ten to 15 percent is standard in restaurants, 50¢ per bag for bellboys, US$1 per day for hotel maids.

TOILETS

Clean and well-maintained public restrooms can be found at shopping malls and most archaeological sites in the region. If there is an attendant, expect to pay a small fee. Men's rooms will be labeled *caballeros*, *hombres*, or 'H'; women's *damas*, *mujeres*, or 'M.'

Where are the restrooms... **Dondé están los sanitarios?**

TOURIST INFORMATION *(oficinas de informacíon turística)*

The following are the addresses of GMTO offices operating outside Mexico.

Canada: 1 Place Ville Marie, Suite 1510, Montréal, Québec H3B 2B5, tel: (514) 871-1052; fax: (514) 871-3825; 2 Bloor Street West, Suite 1502, Toronto, Ontario M4W 3E2, tel: (416) 925-0704; fax: (416) 925-6061; 999 West Hastings Street, Suite 1610, Vancouver, British Columbia V6C 2WC, tel: (604) 669-2845; fax: (604) 699-3498

US: 31 East Street, 3rd Floor, New York, NY 10021, tel: (212) 821-

0314; fax: (212) 821-0367; 300 North Michigan Avenue, 4th Floor, Chicago, IL 60601, tel: (312) 606-9273; fax: (312) 606-9015; 2401 West 6th Street, 5th Floor, Los Angeles, CA 90057, tel: (213) 351-2069; fax: (213) 351-2074; 10440 West Office Drive, Houston, TX 77042, tel: (713) 780-3740; fax: (713) 780-8367; 691 Brickell Key Drive, Miami, FL 33131, tel: (305) 381-6996; fax: (305) 381-8982 **UK**: Wakefield House, 41 Trinity Street, London EC3N 4JD, tel: (020) 7488-9392; fax: (020) 7265-0704

There are two state tourist offices covering the locations in this guide: **Quintana Roo**, Carretera a Calderitas #622, 77010 Chetumal, tel: 983/832-5073; **Yucatán**: Calle 59 #514, 79000 Mérida, tel: 999/924-8386. Tourist information can be found locally at **Cancún** (22 Avenida Tulum, Downtown Cancún, tel: 998/884-8073), **Cozumel** (Plaza del Sol, 2nd floor, Avenida Benito Juárez, tel: 987/872-0972), and **Mérida** (Calle 60 below the Péon Contreras Theatre, tel: 999/924-9290; also in the Governor's Palace).

There are a wide variety of information magazines and brochures available, including the informative *Yucatán Today* for Mérida, and *Cancún Tips* available all over Cancún. Playa del Carmen, Tulum, Akumal and other resorts also have their own information magazines.

W

WEBSITES

Although many websites have been included in 'What to Do' and in other parts of this section, the following will be useful for general background and research before you make your trip. Some also offer links to other more specific sites.

<www.cancunmx.com> is a good place to start planning; <http://go-cancun.com> is the official site of the Cancún Convention & Visitors Bureau; <www.cancunsouth.com> has information about Playa del Carmen, Tulum, and other locations on the Maya Riviera; <www.isla-mujeres.net> is the official website for Isla Mujeres.

Recommended Hotels

The Hotel Zone of Cancún is a modern resort—all the hotels were built after 1970, therefore they are very much alike in terms of amenities and standards. All have air-conditioning, swimming pools, restaurants, and beach access. There are no budget accommodations, but standards rise to luxury, and there are thousands of beds here, with large and small hotels to choose from. Downtown Cancún has more moderate and budget hotels, though it is a short bus ride to the beach. Cozumel and Isla Mujeres both have a range of accommodations from luxury to basic, as does the resort of Playa del Carmen. Mérida, too, has hotels in every price bracket.

The following list covers a range of hotels in all price brackets (price is for a double room in high season; prices in the resorts can be 50 percent lower Apr–Dec).

$$$$$	more than US$260
$$$$	US$180–260
$$$	US$120–180
$$	US$70–120
$	up to US$70

CANCUN

DOWNTOWN

Hotel Cotty $ *Avenida Uxmal No. 44, tel: (998) 884-0550; fax: (998) 884-1319.* Long established, family-run hotel with reasonable rates and amenities, including cable TV, just 100m from the bus station. 28 rooms.

Radisson Hacienda $$$ *Avenida Nader 1 S.M. 2, tel: (998) 881-6500; fax: (998) 884-7954; <www.radissoncancun.com>.* Occupying a building inspired by hacienda architecture, the Radisson

Hacienda has a total of 248 rooms. Mexican and International specialties served at the El Granaro Restaurant.

Kokai Cancún (Howard Johnson) $$ *Avenida Uxmal No. 26, Supermanzana 2-A, tel: (998) 884-3218; fax: (998) 884-4335; <www.hotelkokai.com>.* Small friendly hotel, one block east of Avenida Tulum. Rooms are small but clean. Roof garden with Jacuzzi and first floor swimming pool; restaurant and bar. 48 rooms.

Mexico Hostels $ *Corner Avenida Uxmal/Palmera, tel: (998) 887-0191; <www.mexicohostels.com>.* Very inexpensive hostel with good facilities including internet café, kitchen and lounge area with cable TV. Just four blocks from the bus station. 64 beds including 20 under the rooftop *palapa*. Ideal for backpackers.

El Patio $ *Avenida Bonampak No. 51 & Calle Cereza, tel: (998) 884-3500; fax: (998) 884-3540.* Peaceful, European-style guesthouse with rooms surrounding a lush courtyard. Each room has tiled floors and rustic wood furnishings; some have kitchenettes, and there's also a common kitchen area. 18 rooms

Hotel Parador $$ *Avenida Tulum No. 26, tel: (998) 884-1043; fax: (998) 884-9712; <www.hotelparador.com.mx>.* On Avenida Tulum among the restaurants, gift shops, and travel agents, this budget hotel is clean and its interior relatively modern. Cable TV; small pool at the rear; restaurant/bar on the first floor. 65 rooms.

HOTEL ZONE

Continental Plaza Cancún $$$ *Boulevard Kulkucán, km 11.5, tel: (998) 881-5500; fax: (998) 881-5695.* Attractive Mediterranean-style hotel. The main building has three restaurants and two swimming pools, while the separate villa section has a further swimming pool and two tennis courts among its amenities. 638 rooms in total.

Fiesta Americana Condesa Cancún $$$$ *Boulevard Kulkucán, km 16.5, tel: (998) 881-4200; fax: (998) 885-2014; <www. fiesta americana. com>.* A beautiful hotel with a warm atmosphere and world-class quality and service. Traditional Mexican colors and architecture surround a large pool area that leads down to a wonderful stretch of white sand beach. 506 rooms with all modern facilities.

Hilton Cancún Beach & Golf Resort $$$$$ *Boulevard Kukulcán, km 16, tel: (998) 881-8000; fax: (998) 881-8093; <www.hilton cancun.com>*. This enormous establishment, with buildings styled to resemble Maya pyramids, sits in the southern part of the Hotel Zone. The hotel has its own 18-hole golf course, and there are several swimming pools, two tennis courts, a kids' club and fitness center. 426 rooms.

Meliá Cancún Conference Center and Golf Resort $$$$$ *Boulevard Kukulcán, km 16.5, tel: (998) 881-1100; fax: (998) 881-1740; <www.solmelia.es>*. Beautiful hotel shaped like three pyramids with glass roofs. The man-made waterfalls and fountains and the cascading plants in the huge main interior atrium give the feeling of a Yucatecan *cenote*. Two pools, three restaurants, stores. 450 rooms.

Park Royal Pirámides Cancún $$$$ *Boulevard Kukulcán, km 12.5, tel: (998) 885-1333; fax: (998) 8850113*. A sleek hotel consisting of two pyramid-shaped towers just steps away from La Isla Shopping Center. Rooms have views either of the lagoon or the ocean, and feature pigmented sand artwork designed by famous Mexican artists. 282 rooms.

El Pueblito Beach Cancún $$$–$$$$ *Boulevard Kulkucán, km 17.5, tel: (998) 885-0422; fax: (998) 885-0731; <www.pueblito hotels.com>*. Thoughtfully designed, colorful hotel set along one of Cancún's best beaches. Rooms distributed in 29 low-rise villas decorated with typical Mexican-style elements and with an ocean, pool, lagoon, or garden view. Five swimming pools. 350 rooms.

Villas Tacul $$$$ *Boulevard Kulkucán, km 5.5, tel: (998) 883-0000; fax: (998) 849-7070; <www.villastacul.com.mx>*. This small, secluded hotel is located on the north side of the Hotel Zone, with great views across the water to Isla Mujeres. The hotel consists of 23 tastefully designed villas, with standard rooms and studios, surrounded by lush gardens, all with modern facilities. 79 rooms.

ISLA MUJERES

La Casa de los Sueños $$$$$ *Carretera Garrafón, tel: (998) 877-0651; fax: (998) 877-0708.* Originally a private home, this beautiful building in the south of the island is now an adults-only upscale B&B, catering to the discerning traveler. Rooms are individually designed with high quality in mind. Swimming pool and meditation area. 8 rooms.

Hotel Marcianito $–$$ *Calle Abasolo No. 10, tel: (998) 877-0111.* Pleasant, family-owned hotel in downtown Isla Mujeres, just off the main Avenida Hidalgo. Simple but clean rooms with tiled floors, air-conditioning and TV; shared balconies. 13 double rooms.

Hotel Na Balam $$$–$$$$ *Calle Zazil-Há No. 118, tel: (998) 877-0279; fax: (998) 877-0446; <www.nabalam.com>.* Located on Playa Norte, this hotel has both poolside and beachfront rooms, each with terrace or balcony. Swimming pool and recreation room on site; yoga classes available. Two restaurants including the Zazil Ha, one of the best on the island. 31 rooms.

Hotel Playa la Media Luna $$$, *Punta Norte, tel: (998) 877-0759; fax: (998) 877-1124; <www.playamedialuna.com>.* Located on Half Moon Beach in the northeast of the island, a 2-minute walk from Playa Norte. Nicely appointed rooms, each with its own private balcony overlooking the beach; rooftop terrace with hammocks; pool. 18 rooms.

Villa Rolandi $$$$$ *Carretera Sac Bajo, tel: (998) 877-0500; fax: (998) 877-0100; <www.villarolandi.com>.* Exclusive Mexican-Mediterranean style hotel on the west coast of the island, complete with stone floors and tiled ceilings. All suites have an ocean view, marble bathrooms, and full amenities. The Casa Rolandi restaurant offers a real a gourmet experience. 20 junior suites.

Hotel Secreto $$$$$ *Punta Norte, tel: (998) 877-1039; fax: (998) 877-1048; <www.hotelsecreto.com>.* Small, elegant hotel with striking contemporary architecture in the northeast of the island on Half Moon Beach. Each suite is individually decorated with original artwork and includes CD Sound System and TV with international cable. Private verandas with unobstructed views of the beach and a swimming pool surrounded by lush tropical gardens. 9 rooms.

COZUMEL

Amigo's B&B $–$$ *Calle 7 Sur No. 571-A, San Miguel, tel: (987) 872-3868; fax: (987) 872-3528.* Located on a quiet street five blocks from the ocean, this is a secluded oasis with delightful garden pool and *palapa*-style accommodations. Each room has two single beds and a sofa bed, a kitchenette and private bath. Hammocks supplied.

Colonial Hotel $–$$ *Avenida 5 Sur No. 9, San Miguel, tel: (987) 872-0209; fax: (987) 872-1387.* A simple hotel near the main square. Rooms are clean and have TV and fridge, but they open onto a common corridor; no balconies. Continental breakfast served in the lobby. 20 rooms.

Fiesta Americana Cozumel Dive Resort $$$$ *Carretera Chankanaab, km 7.5, tel: (987) 872-2622; fax: (987) 872-2666; <www.fiestaamericana.com>.* Beachfront resort facing the Palancar Reef and located only minutes from restaurants, shopping, and nightlife. Caters to divers. Pool, restaurant. 228 rooms.

Flamingo Hotel $$ *Calle 6 Norte No. 81, San Miguel, tel: (987) 872-1264; <www.hotelflamingo.com>.* Centrally-located hotel in colonial style, two blocks from the main square and a half block from the waterfront. Rooms have Mexican-style stucco walls and plantation shutters, and there is a lush courtyard and rooftop terrace overlooking the Caribbean. Facilities include cable TV and an internet café. Dive packages available. 22 rooms.

Hacienda San Miguel $$–$$$ *Calle 10 Norte No. 500, between 5th Avenue and the Rafael Melgar, tel: (987) 872-1986; fax: (987) 872-7043; <www.haciendasanmiguel.com>.* Classic colonial-style hacienda hotel in downtown San Miguel with beautifully decorated rooms surrounding lush gardens. Units range from small studios to large suites and include kitchenettes and cable TV. 11 rooms.

Melia Mayan Paradisus $$$$$ *Costera Norte, km 5.8, tel: (987) 872-0411; fax: (987) 872-1599; <www.solmelia. es>*. All-inclusive beach resort 10 minutes north of San Miguel. Many rooms have recently been refurbished. Two restaurants, two pools, watersports, daily activities, kids' club, nightly entertainment. 180 rooms.

Playa Azul Golf & Beach Hotel $$$$–$$$$$ *Carreterra San Juan, km 4, Zona Hotelera Norte, tel: (987) 872-0033; fax: (987) 872-0110; <www.playa-azul.com>*. Exclusive hotel located on the beautiful San Juan beach. All rooms and suites have ocean-view balcony. Swimming pool, three restaurants, beach bar; fishing and diving available; golf at the Cozumel Country Club. 34 rooms and suites.

Presidente InterContinental Cozumel $$$$$ *Costera Sur, km 6.5, tel: (987) 872-9500; fax: (987) 872-9501; <www.cozumel.intercontinental.com>*. Probably the most upscale hotel on the island, the InterContinental is located near Chankanaab Park. Two restaurants, bar, swimming pool, tennis courts, kids' club. 253 rooms.

PLAYA DEL CARMEN

Colibri $$ *1a Avenida Norte between calles 10 and 12, tel: (984) 873-1833, <www.hotel-colibri.com>*. German-run hotel right on the beach, with spacious rooms and peaceful atmosphere; beach restaurant. Offers a choice of large rooms and more traditional cabañas, all simply but tastefully decorated. 28 rooms and 5 cabañas.

Continental Plaza Playacar $$$$ *Avenida Espíritu Santo, tel: (984) 873-0100; fax: (984) 873-0105*. The Continental Plaza dominates the south-central beachfront beyond the pier. The town and beach are on your doorstep, yet you can easily retreat to the hotel if you wish. All modern amenities, two restaurants, pool. 185 rooms.

Copa Cabaña $–$$ *Avenida 5 No. 209, between calles 10 and 12, tel & fax: (984) 873-0218; <www.copacabanaplaya.net>*. Good-value hotel with pleasant, shady courtyard and hammocks outside every room. Massage, Jacuzzi in the courtyard, and gymnasium facilities. Single, double, and junior suite rooms.

Hotel El Faro $$$$ *Calle 10 Norte, tel: (984) 873-0970; fax: (984) 873-0968, <www.hotelelfaro.com>.* One of the best hotels in Playa, facing the beach and incorporating the distinctive 'lighthouse' as its centerpiece. Rooms, tastefully decorated with Mexican art and handicrafts, are tucked away in several two- and three-story buildings amid tropical gardens. Restaurant, *palapa* bar and pool. 28 rooms.

Hotel Lunata $$–$$$ *Avenida 5 between calles 6 and 8, tel: (984) 873-0884; fax: (984) 873-1240; <www.lunata.com>.* Pleasant hotel right on 5th Avenue at the heart of Playa del Carmen, incorporating a mixture of hacienda- and pueblo-style architecture. Rooms are finished to a high standard and include all modern amenities. Pleasant garden at the rear. 10 rooms.

Mosquito Blue $$$–$$$$ *Avenida 5 between calles 12 and 14, tel: (984) 873-1335; fax: 873-1337; <www.mosquitoblue.com>.* One of the first and best hotels in Playa. Beautifully appointed rooms with marble showers and mahogany beds. The restaurant has an inventive menu with Italian twist; the Blue Bar in a *palapa* faces one of the hotel's two pools. No children under 16. 46 rooms and suites.

MÉRIDA

Casa del Balam $$$ *Calle 60, corner Calle 57, tel: (999) 924-2150.* First-class hotel in the heart of Mérida, with beautiful patio gardens and pool. Rooms are elegantly decorated with colonial antiques, wrought iron accessories and marble floors.

Luz en Yucatán $–$$ *Calle 55 No. 499 between calles 58 and 60, tel: (999) 924-0035; <www.luzenyucatan.com>.* Single-story townhouse in the heart of Mérida with tastefully furnished rooms and apartments, and enticing pool. Yoga and other health and fitness activities available; cable TV.

Hotel Medio Mundo $$–$$$ *Calle 55 No. 533 between calles 64 and 66; tel/fax: (999) 924-5472; <www.hotelmediomundo.com>.* Family-operated hotel in a renovated 19th-century mansion. Rooms, each tastefully designed with its own individual features, are ranged around a tranquil, exotically-planted courtyard, and there is a terrace and pool at the back. 12 rooms.

La Misión Fray Diego $$$ *Calle 61 between calles 64 and 66, tel: (999) 924-1111; <www.lamisiondefraydiego.com>.* Fine little hotel in a restored 17th-century residence one block from the historic center, with elegant rooms and wonderful grounds. 20 standard rooms, four special category rooms, and two master suites with Jacuzzi.

Hacienda Xcanatun $$$$ *Carretera Mérida–Progreso, km 12 tel: (999) 941-0213; <www.xcanatun.com>.* A privately-owned small luxury hotel in a restored 18th-century hacienda just north of Mérida. The hotel has a beautifully designed interior, the rooms have all modern amenities, and the cuisine (international and Yucatecan) at the 'Casa de Piedra' restaurant is superb. 18 suites.

UXMAL

The Lodge at Uxmal $$$ *(opposite the site entrance), tel: (997) 971-2102; fax: (997) 976-2102; <www.mayaland.com>.* Pretty hotel blending Maya and European architectural styles, with *palapa* roofs, hacienda-style verandas and locally produced wood furnishings in the rooms. Two pools; open-air restaurant.

Hotel Misión Uxmal $$ *Carretera Merida-Campeche, km 78, tel: (997) 976-2022; fax: (997) 976-2023; <www.hotelmision.com .mx>.* Hotel with views of the ruins at Uxmal, though it is 3km (2 miles) from the site entrance. Large rooms with basic but clean furnishings and balconies; pool; restaurant. 100 rooms.

CHICHÉN ITZÁ

Mayaland Resort $$$–$$$$ *Carretera Mérida-Cancún, km 120, tel: (985) 851-0027; fax: (985) 851-0129.* Just 4km (2½ miles) from the entrance to the site, the Mayaland offers good rooms in the main building and terraced cottages in lush tropical surroundings. Cottages have thatched *palapa*-style roofs and hammocks on the terraces. Three pools; two restaurants; shuttle to the site. 95 rooms.

Recommended Restaurants

Cast aside your preconceptions about Mexican food and make the most of the opportunity to savor the local Yucatecan cuisine. The dishes are often subtle and exotic, influenced by the recipes of the ancient Maya. Fiery heat is an optional extra – chili sauces are served on the side. The best value and variety is to be found out in the Yucatecan countryside, or in downtown Cancún, where you can enjoy local food at a reasonable cost. For plush, stylish restaurants, international cuisine and high prices, or fast food, stick to the Hotel Zone or other resort areas.

In general, reservations are needed only in the more expensive hotel restaurants. Elsewhere it's first come, first served.

Below is a list of restaurants throughout the region. As a basic guide we have used the following symbols to give some idea of the price of a three-course meal for two, excluding drinks:

$$$$$	more than US$50
$$$$	US$40–50
$$$	US$30–40
$$	US$20–30
$	up to US$20

CANCÚN

DOWNTOWN

Los Almendros $$$ *Avenida Bonampak at Sayil, tel: (998) 887-1332*. Los Almendros – a family-run chain that has four restaurants across Yucatán – claims to have invented *poc chuc* (char-broiled pork steak), which has become a standard in modern Yucatecan cuisine. The menu has many delicious regional dishes, described in English and with photographs for guidance. The service is excellent. Open daily 11am–10pm.

La Habichuela $$$ *Carreta Margeritas No. 25, tel: (998) 884-3158.* Set in a Yucatecan home with authentic wooden floors, this small restaurant serves great combination Yucatecan-Caribbean dishes. You can also sit outside in the garden with its Maya ruins special effects. Open daily noon–midnight.

Rolandi's Pizzeria $–$$ *Corner Tulum/Coba, tel: (998) 884-4047.* Simply the best oven-baked pizza and fresh pasta dishes. From the same stable as Casa Rolandi in the Hotel Zone, though with a simpler menu. Open daily 1pm–11.30pm.

HOTEL ZONE

Blue Bayou $$–$$$$, *Hyatt Cancún Caribe Hotel, Boulevard Kukulcán, km 10.5, tel: (998) 848-7800.* Award-winning restaurant on five levels surrounded by a natural tropical garden and waterfalls, and specializing in Cajun, Creole, and international cuisine. Live jazz. Open daily 6.30–11pm.

Captains Cove $$$ *Royal Plaza & Marina, Boulevard Kukulcán, km 16.5, tel: (998) 885-0016.* Seafood restaurant in *palapa*-style setting also serving international dishes such as Angus steak and ribs. Excellent place for buffet-style breakfast (7am–11.30am). You can eat out on the terrace overlooking the lagoon. Open daily 7am–11pm.

Carlos 'n Charlie's $–$$ *Boulevard Kukulcán, km 5.5, tel: (998) 849-4057.* Combines good international and Mexican food with partying, dancing, live music, and lots of fun. House specialty is the BBQ grill. Magnificent views of the lagoon. Open daily noon–3am.

Casa Rolandi Ristorante $$$$–$$$$$ *Plaza Caracol, Boulevard Kukulcán, km 8.5, tel: (998) 883-2557.* Classical northern Italian and Swiss cuisine. Specialties include pastas, meat dishes, pizzas, and bread baked fresh in the wood-burning stove on the premises. Italian wine list; champagne by the glass. Open daily 1–11.30pm.

Fantino $$$$$ *Returno del Rey 36 at the Ritz Carlton Hotel, Zona Hotelera, tel: (998) 881-0808.* This first class restaurant is probably the finest dining experience in Cancún, focusing on creative Italian cuisine with a Mediterranean influence The dining room has crystal chandeliers and furniture reminiscent of 17th-century France. Open Mon–Sat 6.30–11pm

Jonny Rockets $ *La Isla Shopping Village, Boulevard Kukulcán, km 12.5.* 1950s-style diner with great burgers and a wide choice of other treats. Open daily 11am–11pm.

La Dolce Vita $$$–$$$$ *Boulevard Kukulcán, km 14.5, tel: (998) 884-1384.* Said to serve the best Italian food in Mexico, this restaurant is housed in a custom-made building overlooking the lagoon. You can fine-dine on quail's eggs or settle for a simple dish of fresh pasta in one of a range of superb sauces. Seafood also a specialty. Open Mon–Fri 1pm–midnight; Sat–Sun 5pm–midnight.

La Joya Restaurant $$$$ *at the Coral Beach Hotel, tel: (998) 883-2900.* Superb restaurant serving the best in Mexican cuisine. The beautiful dining room is matched by the presentation and service. Good wine list. Open Tues–Sun 6.30–11pm.

Lorenzillo's Lobster House $$–$$$$ *Boulevard Kukulcán, km 10.5, tel: (998) 883-1254.* Palapa-style restaurant with a pretty terrace located by the shallows of the lagoon. The best in fresh seafood, but lobster is the specialty, served all year from the restaurant's lobster farm. Ribs and prime rib roast also on the menu. Open daily noon–midnight.

Mayan Restaurant Pacal $$$–$$$$ *La Mansion-Costa Blanca, Boulevard Kukulcán, km 8.5, tel: (998) 883-2184.* The Maya past and present are artfully entwined in this restaurant. Choose between Yucatecan specialties such as the *relleno negro* and *cochinita pibil* or international dishes like the prime rib, the house specialty. Open daily noon–midnight.

Mikado $$–$$$$ *adjacent to Marriott CasaMagna Resort, Boulevard Kukulcán, km 14.5, tel: (998) 881-2036.* Japanese and Thai cuisine; sushi, sashimi, teppan-yaki, and fragrant Thai soups and curries. Individual tables or shared 'show' tables; features a terrace with spectacular lagoon views. Open daily 6–11pm.

The Plantation House $$$$ *Boulevard Kukulcán, km 10.5, tel: (998) 883-1455.* Caribbean-style cuisine in a beautiful wooden building set on piles over the waters of the Nichupté lagoon. An elegant dining experience. Open daily 5pm–midnight.

Ruth's Chris Steak House $$$–$$$ *Kukulcán Plaza, Boulevard Kukulcán, km 13, tel: (998) 885-3301.* Internationally acclaimed for its prime steak, cooked exactly to your requirements; also try seafood dishes such as the blackened tuna. Open daily 1.30–11.30pm.

ISLA MUJERES

Restaurant-Bar Amigos $–$$ *Avenida Miguel Hidalgo No. 19, tel: (998) 877-0624.* Good Mexican/international cuisine at reasonable prices. Open daily for breakfast, lunch and dinner.

Lorena $$–$$$ *Avenida Guerrero, one block east of Avenida Miguel Hidalgo.* Excellent restaurant with personal service and daily specialties in the pleasant atmosphere of a renovated clapboard house.

La Cazuela M & J $–$$ *behind the church, off the main square, next to Hotel Roca de Mar.* A wide range of Mexican and international cuisine, specializing in *cazuelas* – a cross between an omelette and a soufflé. Great views of the Caribbean. Open daily 7am–2pm.

Rolandi's $–$$ *Avenida Miguel Hidalgo No. 110, tel: (998) 877-0430.* A favorite for visitors for many years. Specializing in great pizzas and garlic bread cooked in a wood-burning stove. Open daily for lunch and dinner.

Zazil-Ha $$–$$$ *Zazil-Ha 118, at the Hotel Na Balam, tel: (998) 877-0279.* Set on the beach of Playa Norte and the hotel terrace, the setting of this restaurant is matched by the delicious fresh food. A good range of dishes, from seafood and pasta to traditional Maya and Mexican. Open daily for breakfast, lunch and dinner.

COZUMEL

El Capi Navegante $$ *Avenida 10 Sur No. 312, San Miguel, tel: (987) 872-1730.* Long-established seafood restaurant; specialties including snapper steak, caribbean buttered lobster, and assorted grilled seafood platter. Open daily 11am–11pm.

Casa Denis $–$$ *Calle 1 Sur No. 132, San Miguel, tel: (987) 872-0067.* Long-established restaurant in a traditional wooden clapboard house just off the main square, serving authentic Yucatecan food, tacos and seafood. Tables outside on the pedestrian-only street and on the shady rear patio. Open Mon–Sat 7am–11pm, Sun 5–11pm.

Guido's $$ *Avenida Rafael E Melgar No. 23 (between calles 6 and 8), tel: (987) 872-0946.* Pizzas cooked in a wood-fire oven for that authentic Italian flavor; succulent pastas served with a variety of sauces. The small entrance leads to a pretty, plant-filled courtyard. Open Mon–Sat 11am–11pm, closed Sun.

Jeanie's Waffle House $ *Avenida Rafael E Melgar next to the Hotel Vista del Mar, tel: (987) 872-6095.* One of the most popular places for breakfast on Cozumel. Waffles, eggs, and hash browns served with a smile. Some Mexican dishes available. Open daily 6am–5pm.

La Cabaña del Pescador $$–$$$ *Carretera Santa Pilar, km 4 (opposite the Hotel Playa Azul), tel: (987) 872-0795.* This restaurant, in a tropical garden setting, serves nothing but fresh lobster tails, sold by weight and cooked to a secret recipe. Open daily 6–10.30pm.

Rock N Java Café $ *Avenida Rafael E Melgar No. 602, tel: (987) 872-4405.* Excellent place for a light bite, featuring delicious vegetarian cuisine and a selection of pies, cakes, pastries, and sandwiches.

La Veranda $$$ *Calle 4 Norte 140 (between avenidas 5a and 10a), tel: (987) 872-4132.* Caribbean restaurant in a traditional wooden clapboard house, creating inventive seafood dishes from tropical ingredients. Pleasant atmosphere; garden at the rear for open-air dining. Open daily 4.30pm–midnight.

PLAYA DEL CARMEN

Las Mañanitas $$$ *Avenida 5 between 4 and 6, tel: (984) 873-0114.* Very pleasant restaurant, part undercover and part on an open terrace, serving excellent Mexican and international cuisine prepared with Italian flair. Friendly service. Open daily 7am–11.30pm.

Hemingway $$$ *Avenida 5 between 12 and 14, tel: (984) 803-0004.* Extremely impressive-looking restaurant on two levels under an enormous open *palapa*. Specializes in Cuban cuisine; live Cuban and salsa music. Open for lunch and dinner.

La Parrilla $$–$$$ *Avenida 5, corner of Calle 8, tel: (984) 873-0687.* Long-established Mexican restaurant specializing in grilled seafood and meats. Mariachi musicians every night, and it does tend to get very busy. Open daily noon–1am.

Yaxche Maya Cuisine Restaurant $$–$$$$ *Calle 8 between 5th and 10th Avenues, tel: (984) 873-2502.* With its fusion of Maya, Yucatecan and European cuisine, served in a 'Maya temple' environment and a garden inspired by the ruins of Tulum, this is one of the most interesting places to eat in Playa. Open for lunch and dinner.

MÉRIDA

Restaurant Amaro $$ *Calle 59 between calles 60 and 62, tel: (999) 928-2451.* Pleasant courtyard restaurant serving vegetarian and whole-food dishes, along with crepes and Yucatecan specialties. Open daily 10am–10pm.

La Bella Epoca $$$ *Calle 60 No. 495 between calles 57 and 59, tel: (999) 928-1928.* Good regional and international cuisine in the pleasant atmosphere of the Hotel del Parque.

Muelle 8 $$$ *Calle 21 No. 141 between calles 30 and 32, tel: (999) 944-5343.* One of Mérida's best seafood restaurants, specializing in fresh Gulf and Caribbean fare and including such classics as *pescado a la Veracruzana* (fish Veracruz style). Open daily 11am–6pm.

INDEX